PBH

AF652510

EDUCATION FOR TWENTY FIRST CENTURY

EDUCATION FOR TWENTY FIRST CENTURY

Edited by

S.P. NAIK

ANMOL PUBLICATIONS PVT. LTD.

NEW DELHI - 110 002 (INDIA)

ANMOL PUBLICATIONS PVT. LTD.
4374/4B, Ansari Road, Daryaganj
New Delhi - 110 002
Ph.: 23261597, 23278000
Visit us at: www.anmolpublications.com

Education for Twenty First Century
© Reserved, 2004
ISBN 81-261-0160-1

[All rights reserved. No part of this publication may be reproduced, stored in a retrieval system or transmitted, in any form or by any means, mechanical, photocopying, recording or otherwise, without prior written permission of the publisher.]

PRINTED IN INDIA

Published by J.L. Kumar for Anmol Publications Pvt. Ltd., New Delhi - 110 002 and Printed at Mehra Offset Press, Delhi.

Contents

Contents

Preface

As twentyfirst century is approaching the teaching-learning process would have different approaches because of easier access to information, the expansion of communications and the impossibility of controlling transborder information and data-flows, the social impact of communication is tremendous.

The present book is designed to impart useful information in the above perspective.

Topics viz. Preparing students for tomorrow's world; Career in class room; Future of small institutions etc. are quite interesting and useful.

I am thankful to all the scholars and authors whose writings are cited or substantially made use of in this book. I am also grateful to Mr. J. L. Kumar for agreeing to publish this book.

—Editor

1

Preparing Students for Tomorrow's World

INTRODUCTION

What kind of education will Americans need in the emerging economy? The conventional view is that Americans will need *more* and *better* education, but there is surprisingly little agreement about what *more* and *better* actually mean. The answer should not depend on occupational projections—that is, on estimates about which jobs are likely to be plentiful should the economy continue in the direction it is now moving—for that direction is toward a continuing decline in the living standard of most Americans. We first need to define where we want our economy to go and then ask what kind of education will help to propel us in that direction.

The purpose of this chapter is to explore where the economy is heading, where it should be heading, and what education can and should contribute. Its modest goal is to provide a framework for continuing discussion about these vital matters. By focusing on the relationship between education and the next economy, I do not mean to suggest that education's only, or most important, purpose is economic. To the contrary: A truly educated person is motivated by, and can find satisfaction, a wide array of things that are not traded in markets or that cost very little. A just and democratic society depends on a citizenry educated in civic responsibility rather than in economic aggrandizement.

The Current Mess

The stock market crashed on October 19, 1987, but the deterioration of the American economy had begun long before. America has been busy consuming more than it has produced. In 1986, for example, the nation generated some $800 billion more in goods and services than it had in the recession year of 1982, but it spent about $900 billion more.

We have been able to ignore this profligacy only because foreigners have kept lending us money, buying our corporations, and purchasing our real estate. By the time of the crash, we were $350 billion in debt, almost one-half of the commercial real estate of downtown Los Angeles (among many other cities) was in foreign hands, and foreign creditors were growing sufficiently nervous about our ability to repay our debts that the dollar was heading downward.

A nation living beyond its means faces precisely the same choice as a person living in the same manner; it may grow poorer, or it may improve its means by becoming more productive. America has been exercising the first option. The steadily declining dollar has rendered more expensive everything we purchase from abroad, in most families, two wage earners are necessary to make ends meet, whereas years ago, one would do; average family size is shrinking; young people are having difficulty affording houses nearly as nice as the homes they grew up in; for the first time since the 1930s the percentage of Americans who own their own homes is declining; over one-fifth of our children are now born into poverty. The average American family is no better off today than it was fifteen years ago, even though American is now living off borrowed funds. Were the borrowing to stop, our standard of living would fall precipitously.

As the present work force matures, moreover, the first option (to grow poorer) becomes ever more likely. The number of American young people is declining while retirees are increasing. By the year 2030, when the proportion of our population 65 years of age and older will nearly have doubled from what it is now, the number of workers supporting each retiree will have dropped from 3.3 to a bit over 2. Unless each remaining worker becomes far more productive than now (or unless retirees continue to work long after retirement age, or unless we allow into America large numbers of new immigrants), our average citizen will have to get by on a much smaller income.

The second option (becoming more productive) has been pursued less vigorously. Our indebtedness to the rest of the world would not be alarming were the proceeds invested in our future productivity, but such has not been the case. Net investment in plant and equipment, as a percentage of gross national product, has been no higher in the 1980s than in the perilous 1970s' supply-side predictions to the contrary notwithstanding. Meanwhile, public investments have lagged. Government spending on commercial research and development has declined 95 percent from its level two decades ago; even when added to private-sector research and development, the total is still less than 2 percent of GNP, lower than comparable research and development expenditures in all other advanced industrial nations. Spending to upgrade and expand the nation's infrastructure–the roads, bridges, ports, tunnels, and communications facilities through which our commerce travels–has dropped from 2.3 percent of GNP two decades ago to 0.4 percent today. Federal support for education, job-training, and preschool care has declined as well.

Thus, while manufacturing productivity has risen slightly as a result of advances in automation and efforts at cutting costs, overall productivity gains, weighed down by slow or negative gains in the increasingly important service sector, have dropped to only 1 percent a year, from over 3 percent a decade before. In the last two years, even a declining dollar has barely helped American producers regain market share from foreigners who continue to supply world markets with relatively cheap, high-quality goods. At this rate the dollar will have to drop significantly lower if the trade balance is to be restored.

Most of the panaceas now being offered by politicians and business leaders are alternative means of growing poorer—for example, allowing the dollar to continue to fall, cutting wages, reducing environmental and safety regulations, slashing welfare expenditures, protecting American goods from foreign competition, and even bringing on a recession. These strategies impose the burden of becoming poorer on different groups of citizens over slightly different periods of time, but their overall effects are much the same. There is no secret to becoming poorer. To repeat: The *only* becoming-richer strategy is to become more productive –adding ever-greater value to the world economy.

Work In The Old Economy

Productivity, however, is no longer simply a matter of making more of what we already make at less cost per unit. To add greater value to the world economy, we have to provide higher quality goods, and tailor our products and services to the particular needs of consumers. This is a new challenge, entailing a very different organization of work.

In the early postwar years, most young people could look forward to jobs requiring only that they be able to learn some relatively simple tasks that could be repeated, over and over. That's because the American economy was organized around economies of scale. The goal was high-volume, standardized production in which large numbers of identical items could be produced over long runs, allowing fixed costs to be spread as widely as possible. Whether it was wheat, steel, or even insurance, the same, overarching rule prevailed: Every step along the production process was to be simple and predictable, so that it could be synchronized with every other step. Productivity was a function of high volume and low cost.

There was little room or need for innovation. Once in a while someone came up with a major invention—e.g., continuous casters for making steel, automobile stamping machines, plastics—but these big breakthroughs were relatively few and far between. Indeed, innovation often was seen as a problem rather than as a solution. Innovation meant changes in products and production processes, and such changes cost money. If the changes happened too often, it was difficult to achieve the economies of scale necessary to pay for them and still make a profit.

Sometimes competitors quietly agreed not to innovate very much for fear of rocking the profitable boat. These were the days when most industries were dominated by a few large companies—the Big Three auto-makers, a handful of steel producers, three or four food processors—who roughly coordinated prices and investments in order to achieve the kind of stability and predictability necessary for vast economies of scale. The tailfins on our cars grew longer, but underneath the hoods the autos remained about the same year after year, and it didn't matter very much which brand you bought.

Under high-volume, standardized production, a few people at the top made all the decisions. They designed the system and planned all the standard operating procedures by which it would run. Most people followed orders. Indeed, for the production system to be stable and predictable, the majority had to follow orders, exactly. Rigid work rules and job classifications posed no challenge to this hierarchical system, because every job was rigid to begin with–like cogs in a wheel.

A primary goal of public education within this stable system was to prepare most young people for such "cog" jobs. They had to be trained to comprehend and accept instructions, and then to implement them conscientiously. Discipline and reliability were core virtues.

A much smaller number of young people had to be prepared to act as decision makers at the top. They needed to be trained to gather information, translate, the information into abstract symbols, manipulate the symbols to find answers, turn the answers into operating instructions, and then communicate the instructions downward. Here, abstract, logic, clarity, and firmness were the core virtues.

Our schools were reasonably effective at preparing Americans for these two kinds of jobs. Most children graduated from high school or vocational school ready to accept cog jobs. A few were set on an advanced track through high school and into colleges that prepared them either for careers as professional managers or for the related professions of law, banking engineering, and consulting. Productivity soared.

Enter The Global Economy

High-volume, standardized production can no longer provide the productivity gains we need to maintain our standard of living. There has been a sea change in the world economy. Beginning in the 1960s and continuing to the present day, the cost of sending things or information around the globe has fallen dramatically. This is a result, principally, of rapid advances in the technologies of transporting and communicating—of innovations such as container ships, satellites, and computers that allowed the production process to be fragmented and parceled out around the globe to wherever pieces of it could be undertaken most cheaply and efficiently. Until recently most goods were produced close to where they were to be consumed; the main exceptions were certain minerals, agricultural goods, and economically unimportant exotica. This pattern has been breaking down at an increasing pace. Consumers of cars, refrigerators, televisions and television programs, insurance policies, and even money, often live in different nations or on different, continents from the producers. The producers, in turn, often depend on far-distant sources for components, designs, and information. It is now often cheaper to ship raw steel across an ocean than across the United States. Slight differences in interest rates may induce a New York corporation to raise money in Tokyo or in Bonn instead of on Wall Street.

Two decades ago international trade hardly figured in the American market; today, more than 70 percent of the goods we produce are actively competing with foreign-made goods. Whoever can do it best and cheapest, anywhere in the world, now sells to whoever is willing to pay the best price, anywhere in the world. The elegant curves of supply and demand that so charm economists are meeting up in the oddest of places.

In a world where routine production is footloose and billions of potential workers are ready to underbid American labor, we can no longer expect to be competitive by simply producing more of the same thing we produced before, at lower cost. As the production of commodities shifts to other nations, America's competitive advantage correspondingly must shift toward work whose value is based more on quality, flexibility, precision, and specialization than on its low.

cost. For example, only a small fraction of the American work force is still employed on the farm. But the food industry nevertheless accounts for close to one-quarter of the jobs in the United States. That's because most of what Americans and consumers in other advanced nations now spend for food goes to the people who process, package, market, and retail it, and to the agricultural epidemiologists, geneticists, international bankers, commodity traders, chemists and process engineers who supply the technology and money for producing it, rather than to those who actually grow and harvest it. Similarly, most of what is spent on appliances, clothing, cars, computers, air travel, or a host of other things is for designing, engineering, fabricating, and advertising, rather than for standardized, routine work. In fact, much of the growth in what has been termed services within the American economy is attributable to just such businesses.

Nor can we hope to be competitive by relying, as before, on major inventions that occur from time to time. These days breakthrough inventions get away. Americans continue to lead the world in big breakthroughs and cutting-edge scientific discoveries. But the big ideas that start in this country now quickly travel abroad, where they get produced at high speed, at low cost, and with great efficiency. All too often, Americans get bogged down somewhere between invention and production. We fail to incorporate new ideas into our products and processes nearly as fast as we should. Several product histories make the point. Americans invented the solid-state transistor in 1947. Then in 1953, Western Electric licensed the technology to Sony for $25,000 —and the rest is history. A few years, later, RCA licensed several Japanese companies to make color televisions—and that was the beginning of the end of color television production in the United States. Routine assembly of color televisions eventually shifted to Taiwan and Mexico. Americans came up with video recorders, basic oxygen furnaces, microwave ovens, and computerized machine tools. But these big ideas and many others found their way into routine standardized production in other nations.

Keeping a technology requires elaborating upon it continuously developing variations and small improvements in it that better meet particular needs. Where innovation is continuous, and products are ever more tailored to customers' needs, the distinction between goods and services further blurs. Thus when robots and computerized machine tools are linked through software that allows them to perform unique tasks, customer service becomes a part of production. When a new alloy is molded to be a specified weight and tolerance, service accounts for a significant part of the value added.

Reports that American workers can no longer compete in manufacturing and must shift to services are thus only half right. More precisely, they can keep high wages only by producing goods with a large component of specialized services, or to state the same thing differently, by providing services integral to the production and use of specific goods. There is no longer any meaningful distinction between the two categories, goods and services.

The point is this: In the new global economy, nearly everyone has access to big breakthroughs and to the machines and money to turn them into standardized products at about the same time, and on roughly the same terms. The only factor or production that is relatively immobile internationally and on which the future standard of living of the nation uniquely depends, is it—our competence, our insights, our capacity to work productively together.

The older industrial economies like America thus have two options: (1) they can try to match the wages for which workers elsewhere are willing to labor, or (2) they can compete on the basis of how quickly and how well they can transform ideas into incrementally better goods and services. Both paths can boost profits and improve competitiveness in the short run, but only the second can maintain and improve the standard of living of most Americans over time.

The Organization Of Work: Two Paths to the Next Economy

The first path—toward stable mass production—relies on cutting labor costs and leaping into wholly new product lines as old ones are played out. For managers this path has meant undertaking (or threatening) massive layoffs, moving (or threatening to move) to lower-wage states and countries, parceling out work to lower-cost suppliers, automating to cut total employment, and diversifying into radically different goods and services. For workers this path has meant defending existing jobs and pay scales, grudgingly conceding lower wages and benefits, shifting burdens by accepting lower-pay scales for newly hired workers, seeking protection from foreign competition and occasionally striking.

The second path involves increasing labor's *value*. For managers this path means continuously retraining employees for more complex tasks, automating in ways that cut routine tasks and enhance worker flexibility and creativity, diffusing responsibility for innovation, taking seriously labor's concern for job security and giving workers a stake in improved productivity via profit-linked bonuses and stock plans. For workers this second path means accepting flexible job classifications and work rules, agreeing to wage rates linked to profits and productivity improvements, and generally taking greater responsibility for the soundness and efficiency of the enterprise. The second path also involves a close and more permanent relationship with other parties that have a stake in the firm—suppliers, dealers, creditors, even the towns and cities in which the firm resides. On this second path, all those associated with the firm become partners in its future, sharing downside risks and upside benefits. Each member of the enterprise participates in its evolution. All have a commitment to its continued success.

The second path requires a fundamentally different organization of work from that which has come before, as well as a different work force within that new organization. The old hierarchical arrangement in which a relatively few well-trained individuals planned and maintained the production system from the top, and almost everyone else undertook cog jobs below, is not up to the challenge. The technologies upon which we must continuously improve, and the tastes to which we must continuously respond, are changing so rapidly that no set of decision-makers at the top can hope to keep up. Much of the relevant information lies below—among production workers, production engineers, sales people and others in direct contact with suppliers, production processes, and customers. There is not enough time for all the relevant information to be passed upward to the top decision-makers and then down again in the form of new operating instructions. With valuable information and expertise dispersed throughout the organization, top managers cannot hope to solve problems and provide answers; their jobs must be to create environments in which people can identify and solve problems for themselves.

Thus the division between workers and managers will blur. Because production is a continuous process of reinvention, efforts will focus on many thousands of small ideas rather than on just a few big ones. Small-scale innovations will occur everywhere in the organization—and must occur quickly and continuously, in response to changing opportunities. One idea should lead to another. Producing the latest generation of automobiles involves making electronic circuits that govern fuel consumption and monitor engine performance; developments in these devices might lead to improved sensing equipment and software for monitoring hart-beats and moisture in the air. Producing cars also involves making flexible robots for assembling parts and linking them by computer; steady improvements in these technologies, in turn may lead to expert production systems that can be applied anywhere. What is considered to be an "automobile manufacturer" thus is transmuted into a broad collection of skills evolving toward all sorts of applications that flow from the same strand of technological development.

Ideally, individual skills are integrated into a group; this collective capacity to innovate becomes something greater than the sum of its parts. Over time, as group members work through various problems and approaches, they learn about each others' abilities. They learn how they can help one another perform better, what each can contribute to a particular project, and how they can best take advantage of one another's experience. Each participant is on the lookout for small adjustments that will speed and smooth the evolution of the whole. The net result of many such small-scale adaptations, effected throughout the organization, is to propel the enterprise forward.

Workers also learn how they can better meet customers' needs: Sales people no longer simply "sell" goods and services. They help customers clarify and redefine what they need, and devise new solutions based upon what the firm might potentially provide. Thus sales people must have a complete understanding of the enterprise's capacity to design and deliver specialized products, and designers and engineers must be equally familiar with sales and marketing. In short, the firm's ability to adapt to new opportunities and capitalize on them depends on the capacities of all of its employees to share information and involve themselves in a systemwide search for ways to improve, adjust, adapt, and upgrade.

As workers add value through judgment and knowledge, computers become tools that expand their discretion rather than further simplify their jobs. Computer-generated information can give workers rich feedback about their own efforts, how they affect others is the prroduction process, and how the entire process can be improved. One of the key lessons to emerge from the General Motors-Toyota joint venture in California is that the Japanese automaker does not rely on automation and technology to replace workers in the plant. In fact, human workers, still occupy the most critical jobs—those where judgment and evaluation are essential. Instead, Toyota uses technology to allow workers to focus on those important tasks where choices have to be made. Under this approach, technology gives workers the chance to use their imagination and their insight on behalf of the company.

The New Educational Challenge

The second path to the next economy—increasing the value of labor rather than cutting its costs—relies, above all, on a work force capable of rapid learning. The most important skills will be transferred informally among workers as they gain experience on the job, rather than gleaned through formal education and training. But the ability to learn on the job will depend on learning skills and attitudes developed long before.

The old system of education mirrored the old organization of production; Most people spent eight to twelve years of their childhood training for cog jobs, while a few were propelled toward top policy and planning positions. The new system must prepare far more people to take responsibility for their continuing education and to collaborate with one another so that their combined skill and insights add up to something more than the sum of their individual contributions.

Today's education is different from what it was two or three decades ago, of course. We surely spend more on education—about $300 billion in 1988 alone, which is almost 7 percent of our total annual output of goods and services, or about the same amount of money we spend on national defense. Between the early 1950s and the mid-1980s, per pupil expenditures in American public schools tripled, as measured in constant dollars (although they have hardly increased at all since then).

And we are getting a lot more education than before: Over 57 million of us are formally enrolled in schools and colleges, with millions more in job training and less formal educational activities. Three-quarters of our adults have completed high school; over 86 percent of younger adults in their twenties have done so—twice the percentage of 1940. Six out of ten of our high school graduates begin some from of more advanced education, and one-quarter of our younger adults have completed four years of college—up from 12 percent as recently as 1960.

The quality of public education also has changed, particularly over the last several years. In 1983, the National Commission on Excellence in Education reported that American schools were failing to educate (23 million adults and 13 percent of our 17-year olds were functionally illiterate); they compared badly with those of our trade competitors (our children came in last in 7 out of 19 academic tests, first or second in none); and they failed to teach our children the basics of American history and culture. In response to this report and to others that followed, broad reforms have been initiated: All but five states have raised the minimum requirement for graduation from high school. Most states have also bolstered math and science curricula. Two dozen states, mainly in the South, have inaugurated comprehensive educational reforms including tightened standards, more academic discipline and higher teacher salaries. Forty states now have programs in technological education; New York even requires all junior high school students to take a year of introductory technology. Efforts have been made to reduce truancy and dropout rates, introduce computer literacy and foreign languages in the early years, establish after-school programs require more basic academic courses for a high school diploma, extend the school year, and enhance job-readiness programs.

There have been modest gains. Although, as we shall see, standardized examinations are questionable criteria of success, they offer useful comparisons. In South Carolina, which in 1984 enacted one of the most comprehensive reforms, average Scholastic Aptitude Test (SAT) scores have risen by 36 points. In Florida, where the high school day has been lengthened, SAT scores have increased modestly over the same period. In New York, which also imposed more stringent academic requirements, scores on the Pupil Evaluation Performance test for third graders rose from 77 to 79 percent. In California, the number of students taking three or more years of mathematics has increased by 15 percent and of science by 20 percent.

But the task has just begun. The gains so far have been small. Education is so central to our place in the new world economy that we will have to do a better job—particularly in two respects: helping all our children to become minimally numerate and literate, and preparing them for jobs involving responsibility and collaboration. The challenge is not simply or even most importantly to provide our children with more education, but to provide them with a different kind of education founded upon new premises about the world they will meet in the future.

Basic Numeracy And Literacy

Although a higher proportion of our young people are better prepared for productive lives than ever before, the worst-prepared third of our young people–disproportionately lower income–are almost totally unprepared. They cannot do simple calculations, understand written directions,or read road signs, charts and maps. And they often lack certain basic information about history, literature, geography, and the natural sciences.

These deficiencies are already affecting American business. When the New York Telephone Company undertook a large-scale recruiting effort in 1987, for example, it found that over 80 percent of its New York City applicants failed entry-level examinations in basic reading and reasoning skills. Some 1,700 of Polaroid's employees—about one-third of the firm's hourly work force—and enrolled in a company program teaching them elementary reading and writing. All told, one of three American corporations now provides some form of basic skills training for its employees. The American Society for Training and Development Study predicts the American industry will have to spend as much as $25 billion yearly on remedial education.

Perhaps we are too impatient—maybe the reforms need more time to take hold. Or perhaps they are inadequate to the task of dealing with all the problems that accompany poverty and broken homes. Twenty-two percent of our children are now born into poverty, up from 15 percent in 1970, and it is projected that 60 percent of today's 3-year-olds will live in a single-parent home before they turn 18.

Or it may be that formal schooling comes too late in the lives of our neediest children, by which time learning habits and attitudes are already firmly established. While there is overwhelming evidence that preschool programs designed to develop the intellectual and social skills of poor children have large payoffs later on, less than one-half of 1 percent of our national spending on education goes to children under the age of six. Or perhaps the reforms have backfired upon the neediest: Stricter promotion and graduation requirements may have prompted more of them to dropout. In many of our largest cities, nearly half fail to raduate. Forty percent of Florida's students drop out, as do almost half of Louisiana's Overall, between, 15 and 25 percent of our young people never finish high school.

Whatever the cause, raising the lowest achievers to minimal levels of productive competence is a large part of the challenge of American education in the next economy. Not only do we need a larger population of productive people to help pay off our international debt, but we also need them to support a growing population of retirees.

Responsibility

Achieving basic numeracy and literacy is only part of the challenge. If our economy is to transform itself—if we are to take the second path, toward higher-value production—we can no longer train the majority of our young people for cog jobs requiring primarily discipline and reliability. They must be prepared to take advantage of whatever opportunities present themselves for improvements in product and process. To recognize such opportunities, they must be educated to think critically and to continually learn on the basis of new data and experience.

In some respects, the training of young people in the old economy resembled the system of high-volume, standardized production in which they were to take part when their training was complete: Responsibility was exercised by a very few, at the top. The majority of students were pushed, as if on an assembly line, through a preestablished sequence of steps. Each step involved particular routines and practices. Teachers—the production workers—had little discretion over what they had to do to each batch that passed through; students passively received whatever was doled out. Inspectors tried to weed out the defects, sometimes returning them to an earlier step for reworking. Most got to the end of the assembly line, more or less ready to take their places along real assembly lines somewhere in the economy.

The premises of education in the next economy must be quite different. Just as productivity can no longer be a matter of making more of what we already make at less cost per unit, productivity in education cannot be solely a function of the numbers of children who pass standardized examinations at a lower cost per unit.

Because our future economy will depend to an ever greater extent on thinking rather than repeating learned information, future reforms must motivate teachers and students alike to love learning, and not prescribe to them exactly what should be learned and how and when the information should be doled out. Responsibility must be pushed downward, to students, and teachers. They must be allowed and encouraged to take more initiative in deciding what is learned, and when and how it is learned. Education modelled around long lists of facts that "every adult should know" and standardized tests will produce robots adept at Trivial Pursuit but unable to think for themselves or to innovate for the future.

First, instead of giving students information along a preestablished sequence of steps, and then asking them to "play back" the information tests, the emphasis in teaching should be on educating young people to formulate problems and questions for themselves. Thus, rather than teach students to assume that problems and solutions are generated by others (as they were under high-volume, standardized production) students should be taught to understand that problems and questions are created, that students can have an active role in creating them, and that such critical and creative approaches can guide them through their careers.

Second, instead of teaching through repetition and drill the emphasis should be on allowing students to experiment for themselves with solving the problems they held define. Thus, rather than conveying particular pieces of information or imposing established routines—a type of teaching and learning relevant to high-volume, standardized production—teachers must help students gain the experience of working through problems, and thus discovering underlying principles that help define and solve related problems.

The difference between absorbing information and gaining understanding depends on how much responsibility students are taught to accept for their own continuing learning. It is like the difference between learning how to get from on location to another in a city by having someone drive you or by driving yourself with a guide sitting beside. In the first instance you may eventually learn the way, but you probably will learn sooner by being in the driver's seat. Indeed, if your guide also allows you to experiment a bit, warning you only when you're going down blind alleys or heading in the wrong direction, you may gain even more understanding of the terrain and thus, learn how to find other places as well.

A understanding of underlying principles and patterns allows discovery of other information,. and gives that new information added context and meaning. The new information, in turn, permits deeper insight into the principles and patterns. As Michael Polanyi has written, "[w]e cannot comprehend the whole without seeing its parts, but we cannot see the parts without comprehending the whole."

The habits and techniques of experimentation—of iterative discovery of parts and wholes—will be critical in the next economy, where technologies, tastes, and markets are likely to be in constant flux. Informal, on-the-job education will be a central aspect of work. Formal education and training will no longer be limited to young people, but will be available on a continuing basis to workers throughout their working lives—an accepted and expected aspect of one's career. A work force capable of taking responsibility for its own continuous learning will prove a more precious national asset than countless new factories and equipment.

Collaboration

Specialized skills also will be needed, of course. More of our young people will have to be able to communicate in foreign languages (for every American who now speaks Japanese, there are at least ten Japanese who speak English) and gain a working knowledge of foreign nations and cultures. More of them will need advanced education in mathematics, science, and engineering. (Despite a growing need, fewer bachelor's degrees were awarded in science and engineering in 1987 than on average during the 1970s). There will be a greater need for people who can cross disciplines—from, say, physics to computer programming, from biology to Chinese language and culture.

But our culture has never had much difficulty educating the most talented and fortunate fifth of our young people to do complex intellectual tasks. Analytically sophisticated students already graduate from our universities, trained for narrow specialities in which they manipulate symbols and concepts in wonderous ways. We may want to change the mix somewhat—more engineers and foreign experts, fewer lawyers and financiers—but there is no fundamental problem mustering talented people and getting them educated. The greater challenge is to transfrm the individual talents and specialized skills of the top 20 percent into collective capacities broadly shared across American enterprise.

In the old economy, a relatively few people at the top could analyze and plan the production process by themselves, and then issue operating instructions to everyone else. So long as professional managers and their professional aides—bankers, lawyers, accountants, and engineers—go it "right" on paper, it was assumed that the rest would follow automatically. But paper professionals are far less relèvant to the future. As we have seen, the weakest link in the American economy is between ideas and implementation, between paper and product. Thus if our business enterprises are to be as flexible and innovative at all levels as they need to be, our youngsters must be prepared to work with a through large numbers of people. While there will always be a need for a certain number of solo practitioners, the more usual requirement will be that combinations of individual skills are greater than their sums. Most of the important work will be done by groups, rather than by individual experts.

Learning to collaborate suggests a different kind of education than one designed to prepare a relatively few talented young people to become professional experts. Instead of emphasizing the quiet and solitary performance of specialized tasks, a greater emphasis should be placed on interactive communications linked to group problem-definitions and solutions. Students should learn to articulate clarify, and then restate for one another how they determine questions and find answers. Rather than be trained to communicate specialized instructions and requests—skills relevant to high–volume productions—students should learn how to share their understandings, and build upon each others' insights.

Communication skills are only one aspect of collaboration. Young people also must be taught how to work constructively together. Instead of emphasizing individual achievement and competition, the emphasis in the classroom should be on group performance. Students need to learn how to seek and accept criticism from their peers, to solicit help, and to give credit to others, where appropriate. They must also learn to negotiate—to articulate their own needs, to discern what others need and see things for others' perspectives, and to discover mutually beneficial outcomes.

The "tracking "system, by which students are grouped in the classroom according to the speed of their learning, is another vestige of high-volume, standardized production—the deluxe models moving along a different conveyor belt from the economy cars. This may be an efficient way to cram information into young minds with differing capacities to absorb it; but tracking or grouping can also reduce young peoples' capacities to learn from and collaborate with one another. Rather than separate fast learners from slow learners in the classroom, all children, (with only the most obvious exceptions) should remain together, so that class unity and cooperation are the norm. Faster learners would thus learn how to help the slower ones, while the slower ones would be pushed harder to make their best effort.

In sum, it is not enough to produce a cadre of young people with specialized skills. If our enterprises are to be the scenes of collective entrepreneurship—as they must be—experts must have the ability to broadly share their skills and transform them into organizational achievement; and others must be prepared to learn from them.

The Danger Of Fragmentation

Numeracy, literacy, responsibility and collaboration: this is a tall order for public education. But it is a necessary one if we are to succeed in the world economy in coming years. It will require that we do in our schools what we must do in our business enterprises: push responsibility downward toward teachers and students; invite continuous, incremental innovation at all levels; foster collaboration among parents, teachers, principals, community groups, and the private sector; and encourage flexibility.

Meeting the challenge also requires that we invest substantially in one another. We will have to pay more to educate our children—especially to attract and retrain talented teachers to do the educating. Between 1987 and 1993, American schools must recruit some 1.3 million new teachers—over half of the current force. According to present trends, the labor market will not meet this need. The choice will be either to lower recruitment standards or to raise teachers, salaries. The former choice will be far more costly to the nation than the latter. (It is worth nothing in this regard that starting pay for Japanese school teachers exceeds that for any other public servants in Japan, and is higher than or equal to that of engineers.) Teachers and educational administrators, in turn, will have to accept even more accountability.

We also will have to bear more of the cost of educating our fellow citizens before and after their formal schooling. If ou. children are to be adequately prepared for school, Head Start and other preschool programs for ages 3 and 4, day care for toddlers, must become the norm. If our older workers are to be adequately prepared for jobs that are continuously changing, they must have easy access to retraining and continuing education.

Do we have the will to make the need investments and undertake the necessary changes? Much depends on the extent to which we consider ourselves one people whose fates are linked.

I have before emphasized our choice of path toward the next economy—either cutting labor costs or increasing labor value. The first path will result in a lower standard of living for most Americans; the second requires that we all sacrifice in the short-term in order to reap long-term gains. It should be noted, however, that the fates of our most talented and fortunate citizens are not necessarily linked to the educational attainments of the rest. The new world economy makes it possible for the top fifth of our population to sell their expertise directly in the global market, and thus maintain their standard of livings and that of their children, even as that of other Americans declines. Improvements in the technologies of communications and transportation are facilitating the development of global corporations, partnerships, and consulting businesses that transcend the organization of production within any single nation. The most talented and fortunate fifth—sitting astride these global businesses—are thus losing any unique connection to the American economy.

There are signs that a two-tier society is already developing. Increasingly, our largest, cities are inhabited by paper professionals at the top—lawyers, financiers, consultants, managers—and by unskilled service workers at the bottom—sales clerks, fast–food employees, custodians, hospital orderlies, cab drivers. Nationally, the gap appears to be widening. For 80 percent of American families, the last decade was a time of declining real income. But the wealthiest fifth of our population experienced no decline. In fact, the richest tenth enjoyed an increase of about 16 percent; the top twentieth an increase of 23 percent; and the real income of America's richest 1 percent rose 50 percent. Since 1980 the median income of a married couple, each of whom has had five or more years of education beyond high school has risen to $61,130; the median income of a couple with only high school degrees has risen more slowly, to $36,888. Since 1980 the bottom fifth of the income distribution has lost, on average, one dollar out of every six in earnings, while the top fifth has increased its share of total national income by 8 percent.

Without the active support of the most talented and fortunate fifth of our population, however, it will be difficult to muster the political will necessary to change the present direction. But unless we change, the gap between the top fifth and the rest of us will widen further; and most Americans will continue to grow poorer. There in lies one of the sharpest dilemmas of our time.

2

Missing Educational Reform Agenda

America recurrently attempts to reform its schools. The most recent reform movement gained its momentum from a number of reports and studies about American education that began to gain public attention in 1983 with the publication of the National Commission on Excellence in Education's *A Nation at Risk*. To the surprise of many, the movement is not only still alive but has progressed, at least in some states and communities, beyond its essentially regulatory beginnings to concerns that address fundamental and enduring weaknesses in our schools. Indeed, should those who seek to ride the "second wave" of educational reform be successful, our schools will be better than they have ever been.

While improvements in our schools are being made, our needs and expectations are accelerating. Thus, the changes that are being achieved will probably seem inadequate. Because this could lead to the idea that "we've done what we can reasonably do," or to more cynical conclusions about the futility of investing in public education, the chance to do what needs doing will be lost for the foreseeable future unless we expand the agenda.

There are two general reasons why the current reform agenda is incomplete. First, the proposals that compose the second wave reforms are encumbered both by an undertow of first wave proposals and assumptions and by stated justifications for significant proposals that are unlikely to gain popular support. Second, even if this undertow could be overcome, and political support for the advocated changes developed, the second wave proposals now on the policy agenda fail to address two major problems: (a) the separation of schools and families and (b) the need to develop, beyond the goals policy makers have heretofore owned, the cognitive *capabilities* of our young people.

To argue that the first and second waves will come up short raises the question: short of what? The success of the case I am trying to build depends on the ultimate purposes of education reform to which one subscribes. I believe that two of the most important goals of educational reform should be:

1. significantly improving the performance of low-achieving students so as to narrow the current gap in academic learning between them and high-achieving youngsters and eliminating the inequalities of opportunity and condition that result from that deficit; and

2. developing among almost all children greater interest in and cognitive capacity for learning, "higher-order thinking," and problem solving.

Tall orders, these. It would be possible to compile considerable data to demonstrate that we are a long way from achieving these goals, but I assume that both this reality and the desirability of these goals need no validation.

The First Wave of Educational Reform

While the first wave has not yet broken on the shores of all states—much less all school systems—and may not reach some schools at all, it does seem possible to identify its major concerns, themes, achievements, and limitations.

The Fundamental Assumption of the First Wave

For several years preceding the 1980s, public and policymakers were bombarded with information about declining test scores, the low achievement levels of American students compared to the students of other nations, conflict resulting from desegregation, the debate over prayer in the schools, and other social controversies. The public mind was not so much shaped as it was mirrored by the hyperbole of the 1983 report of the National Commission on Excellence in Education, *A Nation at Risk,* whose title became the rationale of the first wave reforms. It seemed easy to argue that at least part of our problem resulted from the nation's preoccupation with equal opportunity rather than high standards. Accordingly, Wave 1 policies and initiatives paid little attention to students who were physically, mentally, or environmentally handicapped, and federal spending for programs serving such children declined (National Coalition, 1895).

While many who could influence educational policy were concluding that our schools' effectiveness was at a new low, there was, in fact, little evidence that this was so (Hawley, 1985). Indeed, while test scores most relevant to measuring student achievement had declined somewhat in the 1960s and early 1970s, most measures of student learning were on the way up by the mid-1970s (Congressional Budget Office, 1987). In spite of this fact, even most of those who knew better decided to ride the wave to obtain more resources for schools.

Thus the first wave of reform was energized by a conviction that we had fallen from a higher state of grace to a desperate situation that threatened not only individual school children but the nation's economic and military security. As one of the more widely cited passages of *A Nation at Risk* put it:

> If an unfriendly foreign power had attempted to impose on America the mediocre educational performance that exists today, we might well have viewed it as an act of war. As it stands, we have allowed this to happen to ourselves. We have even squandered the gains in student achievement made in the wake of the Sputnik challenge. We have in effect, been committing an act of unthinking, unilateral educational disarmament. (National Commission, 1983, p. 3)

The logical response to such a conclusion was to quickly and forcefully repair the sinking vessel, chart a simpler course, and insist that the sailors the nation's teachers—shape up or ship out. Thus, while the flood of reform proposals that burst upon the schools in the mid-1980s had many currents, most reflected the view that change would come only by a combination of regulations and incentives that would tell educators what to do and insist that they work smarter and harder. (For a specification of first wave proposals, see Passow, 1987.)

Consequences of Wave 1

Empirically grounded reports on the impact of Wave 1 reforms are limited; it seems fair to say that it is too early to tell what the results will be overtime. Public spending for schools has apparently increased more rapidly than one would have predicted from trend lines and increases in the cost of living (Stern, 1988, Chart 1.12), with much of the new money going to improve teachers' salaries. There is reason to believe that the number and academic ability of whites who want to be teachers has increased (Hawley, Goldman, & Austin, 1988).

At this point, the impact of reforms on student achievement cannot be clearly discerned. More students do appear to be taking more math and science courses in high school, and curricula have been aligned with standard tests in many places. Some observers believe that increased emphasis on academic courses and greater use of retention practices have increased the high school drop-out rate, but there is little evidence that this is so, at least in the aggregate (Stern, 1988, Chart 1.8).

Almost everyone who has written about the reforms agrees that, taken together, these measures have reduced discretionary decision-making for school boards, school administrators, and teachers. In particular, a number of the critics of the reform movement point to the "mechanization" and "routinization" of teaching as the most unhappy consequence of the Wave 1 reform efforts (e.g., Wise, 1988, and McNeil, 1986).

Simplification, prescription, and performance measurement were the policy mechanisms that were most common to Wave 1 reforms. Those who believed that schools' problems could be traced to low standards for students and teachers and a lack of focus on academic achievement felt these strategies were sensible. But others, who diagnosed the problems differently, charged that the reforms, on the whole, limited the prospects for quality education by oversimplifying the solutions and restricting rather than facilitating basic changes.

The Wave 1 reforms not only centralized authority for educational policymaking, thus increasing rules and regulations, they reinforced the climate of distrust that had initially motivated the reforms. Moreover, many policy-makers riding the first wave apparently assumed that the problem was to right the ship and get it *back* on course rather than working to streamline the prow, add more sail, or reorganize the command structure. Thus the first wave did not add new capacity to our educational system or try to take on fundamental problems that diminished and constrained the intellectual capacity of children.

The Second Wave

Some believed in the necessity of the first wave reforms but recognized that the reforms were both limited and limiting. This recognition, combined with a concern for a likely shortage of qualified teachers, a worsening trade deficit, and the pent-up energies of would-be reformers who had been waiting for a wave they felt better about riding than the first, gave rise to a second set of priorities for educational improvement. This does not mean that the energy of the first wave is spent. Indeed, it is precisely because the two waves overlap, and sometimes move in different directions, that the potential benefits of the reform movement are so problematic.

The origins of the second wave of reform proposals can be traced to a series of studies that captured considerable attention, at least among those most concerned about improving the nation's schools. *Time for Results,* prepared by the National Governors' Association in 1986, represented both the political ascendance of educational issues and efforts to broaden the reform agenda. The two reports of the Committee for Economic Development, *Investing in Our Children* (1985) and *Children in Need* (1987), represented a growing awareness of the link between economic prosperity and education and, more importantly, an effort to restore the problems of children with special needs to the nation's list of priorities for public spending. The report of the 1986 Carnegie Forum on Education and the Economy drew attention to the importance of effective teaching to effective schools and added the professionalization of teaching and the related restructuring of schools to the reform agenda.

The second wave of reform gained additional momentum from other studies and reports, all of which suggested a need to go beyond the essentially regulatory steps that characterized the major thrust of earlier proposals. But, perhaps because Wave 2 proposals have tried to focus our attention on the need to reach shores we have not yet reached, the calls for change it encompasses have been less energy and more diffuse. Thus the roar of the second wave is less distinct than that of the first and its pull less clearly felt by policymakers and the public at large.

The Second Wave Agenda

The second wave appears to have two main emphases that differ from Wave 1 proposals for school improvement. The first of these¾the concern for addressing the needs of "children at risk" because of poverty, poor physical or mental health, or family instability calls for recommitment to a spate of social programs and, in particular, for preventive policies that address the needs of prospective parents and preschool children. Let me refer to this set of policies as "investment in children strategies."

The other set of second wave reform efforts, which I will call the "investment in teaching strategies," has two complementary but not necessarily dependent emphases. The first centres on attracting and retaining effective teachers, with particular concern for increasing the proportion of academically talented persons in the teaching corps. The policies derived from this goal link readily with first wave reforms: reform of teacher education, higher overall salaries, higher standards for entry to teaching, and differentiated staffing, with higher pay for teachers who manifest exceptional performance and/or are willing to take special responsibility. It is the second focus of the investment in teaching strategies that makes this set of policies second wave: improved working conditions and greater professional discretion for teachers combined with (a) the restructuring of schools to provide teachers opportunities to define and administer school policy and (b) school site management¾the devolution of greater authority over curriculum, instructional strategies, and resource allocation to the school level.

Other proposals might be thought of as second wave reforms including the reform of undergraduate college education and the need to make better use of technology to enhance learning but they do not appear to be high on the political agenda.

Likely Outcomes of the Second Wave

It is difficult to assess the impact of the first wave, predicting the consequences of the second is even more speculative. But making such predictions can serve two purposes: first, identifying obstacles to these reforms may contribute to efforts to overcome them; and, second, such speculation can reveal that the policies being proposed are importantly incomplete.

In assessing the potential outcomes of second wave reforms, we should characterize their political consensus and technical certainty. Political consensus how desirable a given policy is among those with the resources and interest to shape the decision to enact and implement that policy is the product of several factors. Two that seem most important are the extent to which (a) it is perceived that a given problem has both direct and indirect consequences for large numbers of people and (b) how the potential solutions to the problem fit prevailing values about the appropriate role of government in a given policy arena.

By "technical certainty," I mean the confidence one can have about the extent to which the policy can bring about the desired outcome. Certainty depends, among other things, on the strength of the demonstrated cause-effect relationships and the capacity of the individuals and institutions involved to maximize the predicted outcome.

The probability that the chance a given policy will be enacted and effectively implemented is affected, of course, by the amount of money it will require. As the amount required grows, so does the degree of political consensus and technical certainty required. Moreover, as the amount of money required to implement a policy increases, the more the test of technical certainty will take the form of implicit or explicit estimates of return on investment. Technical and political concerns are, of course, interrelated.

Wave 2 Proposals for Investing in Children

I have already suggested that such political consensus that will result in new or reinvigorated programs for children at risk appears to be developing. This consensus transcends conventional divisions between liberals and conservatives, though specific mechanisms to implement programs may yet prove divisive. Advocacy groups like the Children's Defense Fund (1984) are finding support for children at risk among governors, corporate executives, chief state school officers, teachers' organizations, constituent members of the Education Commission of the States, and conservative members of Congress. These support groups are aware of the severity of the problems many children face, realize that society will depend increasingly on those who have traditionally been least well-educated and most prone to social pathologies, and are convinced that the growing evidence of technical certainty of some child investment policies is high (Committee for Economic Development, 1987; Baumeister, Dokecki, & Kupstas, 1987).

Space does not permit a detailed analysis of policy options for addressing all of the problems of children at risk, but three general propositions seem reasonable. First, if we expect to succeed with the set of child investment strategies, we must see them as a set. Preventative policies aimed at reducing the incidence of low birth weight and infant malnutrition and poor health respond to easily understood problems with high and relatively certain benefit/cost ratios. However, it is wishful thinking to suppose that we can "intervene" early in children's lives and, in effect, inoculate them against the forces that will later impede their cognitive and social development. The pathologies associated with poverty, family instability, and community disorder continue to influence children as they grow to young adulthood. Because the technical certainty of extant programs for older children is much lower than for those programs aimed at younger children and because some older children with special needs engage in antisocial behavior, political consensus to support a comprehensive child investment strategy is difficult to obtain.

A second generalization about child investment programs is that they are the responsibility of multiple public agencies and that no institution other than the child's family is in a position to ensure adequate attention to the needs of children at risk. Obviously, when families are unstable or lack the resources to make demands on the various institutions on which their children must depend, children's needs go unmet. Many children have special needs *because* of their situation. This problem is confounded when private services are available because the exit of wealthier families from public service providers reduces the effectiveness of parents' demands for improved public services (Hirschman, 1970).

A third generalization about investment in children programs is that their success with the possible exception of those aimed at nutrition and illness prevention depends on the persons delivering the service. Formula treatments for children with multiple problems are seldom effective; rather, the therapy needed must be determined through diagnoses that take into account the changing circumstances and needs of the child being served. Ideally, the service provider must be intelligent, flexible, and committed and must serve only a small number of children. But because service providers cannot be with children continuously, the most successful programs for children with special needs are those in which parents are trained (and reinforced continuously) to provide the service needed. This, in turn, means that children from stable and well-educated families would profit most from investment in children's programs, though the children who most need such programs often do not have stable and well-educated families.

Wave 2 Proposals for Investing in Teaching

Policies related to the qualities of teachers. Policies aimed at securing certain qualities in our teachers—such as screening devices, salary increases, and so on —are logically related to the outcomes desired, although there is little hard evidence to link specific teacher qualities and student performance (Evertson, Hawley, & Zlotnik, 1985). Of course, the high cost of implementing teacher salary policies limits how much will be done in most places. While most recognize the desirability of attracting and retaining teachers of higher quality however defined), they are unclear as to the technical certainty of the strategies to achieve this goal. Not surprisingly, policies have proliferated that screen out people without the qualities we want. The policies are certain (in the sense that screening is effective), and they don't cost much. Because of the high cost of across-the-board salary increases, we have witnessed policymakers' pursuit of ways to stratify teachers by performance and responsibility so as to focus the largest salary increases on limited number of teachers. This strategy, however, seldom has been accompanied by changes in the organizational structure of schools that actually differentiate teacher functions. This is one reason why so-called ladder plans appear to be unstable wherever they have been introduced. Some proponents of significantly increasing the salaries of teachers argue that much of the money needed to finance such a policy could be obtained from the reallocation of funds now allocated to other educational expenditures (Carnegie Foundation, 1986). But such reallocation proposals weaken the political consensus needed to obtain support for increasing teacher salaries.

Most agree on the desirability of increasing teacher salaries (Gallup, 1987; Louis Harris, 1986), but they are uncertain about its efficacy. There is evidence that increasing teacher salaries will increase the supply of teacher candidates (Kershaw & McKean, 1962), but what a given teacher salary increase will buy in enhanced teacher quality is unknown. Indeed, there is some popular suspicion, reinforced by the emphasis teachers and parents place on the importance of "Mrs. Jones's" love for children in explaining why she is a good teacher, that paying teachers very well would attract the wrong kind of people to the profession. Moreover, it is easy to believe that our teachers should be literate and of above-average intelligence, but it is not clear how literate or how much above average in intelligence teachers must be to facilitate student learning (Evertson et al., 1985). While I know of no direct studies on the questions, it seems likely that most people do not *expect* the average teacher to be as bright as the average engineer, doctor, lawyer, or successful businessman and thus will not think it necessary to pay teachers accordingly.

Another reason for the technical uncertainty of teacher salary increases is that Americans may believe that their children's future success is shaped less by their education than by upbringing, luck, contacts, peer and community influences, and innate ability. For example, Stevenson, Lee, and Stigler (1986) found that American mothers were much more likely than Japanese or Chinese mothers to attribute their child's success in school to innate ability than to effort.

Policies relating to the restructuring of schools. The political and technical limits of regulatory policies and salary increases, coupled with evidence showing that the opportunity to help others learn, is a powerful incentive for people to enter and stay in the profession (Hawley & Rosenholtz, 1984, chap. 3), have given rise to proposals to change the structure of schools and the roles of teachers in ways that would allow talented teachers to maximize their effectiveness and attract and retain talented people in teaching.

However, these proposals, which I will label "restructuring," face considerable difficulties. On the one hand, restructuring proposals are often ambiguous, and the language and symbols they invoke do not promise to foster sufficient political consensus to achieve widespread change. On the other hand, the technical certainty of these proposals is considerably less obvious to those who have not joined the bandwagon than to their advocates. The lack of consensus, of course, contributes to technical uncertainty. Let me elaborate on each of these points.

Like change in general, restructuring in the abstract is a popular idea. But current discussions suggest that those affected by restructuring like the idea only if it does not portend a loss of authority, status, or discretion for them. Proven models of restructured schools do not dot the landscape. Such schools exist, of course, but they are treated in the literature as aberrations that thrive because of unusual circumstances or because of exceptional leadership either among teachers or principals (the latter usually get the credit).

The most common theme in the calls for restructuring is teacher "empowerment." Aside from the vagueness of term, there are at least five reasons why the idea is unlikely to generate much political consensus.

- The first wave of reform rested heavily on the idea that many teachers are incompetent or not hard-working.
- Research and commentary on effective schools frequently emphasizes the importance of strong leadership from the school principal.
- Many school administrators have seen themselves in adversarial relations with teachers, a position complicated by their increased responsibilities for teacher evaluation.
- Many parents appear to feel that teachers already have too much power. For example, more than 50 percent of parents nationwide believe that parents should have more say in curriculum and 5 percent believe they should have less; more than 40 percent of parents believe they should have more say over instructional materials and the types of books available in the school library and only 10 percent believe they should have less (Gallup, 1987, p.21).
- Even a good many teachers seem to be doubtful about the desirability of significantly changing the relative

authority they have vis-a-vis school administrators (Bacharach, Bauer, & Shedd, 1986).

If teacher empowerment is the most common theme of restructuring, the most commons rationale for restructuring seems to be to make teaching "a true profession." But here again the symbol may not be a rallying cry that appeals to many who have not historically advocated more status for teachers. Two decades ago, for example, the professionalization of public sector jobs was seen as a problem because it allegedly distanced public servants from those they were to serve. The product of this concern was proposals for educational vouchers, community school boards, parent advisory councils, and more accountability. And, while professionals such as doctors and lawyers are often envied and paid well, sizable numbers of us speak of the impersonality of physicians and the self-interest of lawyers, traits we do not seek in teachers. Moreover, it is not common to think of a heavily unionized work force and most teachers are union members as professionals.

Proposals for school site management seem to be making little progress largely because they directly confront the centralizing and standardizing effects of the first wave reforms. Moreover, international comparisons, which drove our collective awareness of the need for change, led the pundits, including many political leaders, to conclude that central direction, a uniform curriculum, and the like, held the answer to our problems. In 1987, the Gallup Poll showed that a whopping 84 percent of the American citizens favored having the *federal government require* local districts to meet minimum educational standards (Gallup, 1987, p. 23.)

Some critics of the first wave marveled at how quickly Americans (or at least their elected representatives) seemed to abandon presumably cherished traditions of local control over education. But the power of the first wave to swamp localism suggests that the commitment was not deeply rooted and that our thinking about educational authority had not adapted to changes in the diversity and mobility of our populations. Moreover, the successful efforts to ensure civil rights and civil liberties in our schools had not been rationalized with the value of local control (Ravitch, 1986), and the very foundations of local control—local school boards—had been substantially weakened (Institute for Educational Leadership, 1986).

In short, the justifications given for restructuring often seem to focus on improving the status, autonomy, and income of teachers, and on decentralizing educational decision-making generally. It seems likely that many school board members, school administrators, parents, first wave reformers, and other citizens may have trouble understanding why this will improve student learning. Which brings us to the question of technical certainty of restructuring.

The problem in knowing about the technical certainty of restructuring is that the case for its effects must be largely inferential. It is not that we have not tried restructuring. Many school systems experimented with "differentiated staffing," and "alternative schools" once flourished with the support of federal funds. But research analyzing the effects of these experiments on students is scarce, and the uncertain efficacy of these efforts is suggested by their high mortality rate.

Will restructuring lead to improved student performance? It is possible to conclude from extant research that the conditions identified with restructuring are associated with high student achievement (Hawley & Rosenholtz, 1984). But apparently there are no careful before and after studies of student achievement in restructured schools. It is possible, therefore, that schools with high-achieving students can be structured differently and attract teachers with different qualities. In other words, the directions of the causal arrows are unclear.

If restructuring will lead to improved student achievement, and, on balance, it seems that it will, it will be for one or more of four reasons: (a) the mix of teacher qualities will be different, (b) teachers will be more motivated to do what they know how to do, (c) teachers will be able to do better the things they know how to do, or (d) the opportunities for peer and administrative support will allow teachers to improve their competence.

Those who assert that restructuring will lead to higher teacher salaries argue that restructured schools will attract teachers with qualities society will want to reward more generously. The available evidence does not clearly show this. A competing hypothesis is that if restructuring does attract teachers with desirable qualities, the perceived need to increase salaries will be reduced, since there is some evidence that the conditions associated with restructuring are also associated with teacher job satisfaction and retention (Hawley & Rosenholtz, 1984 chaps. 2-3). While there is no research on the effects of these conditions on teachers with different qualities, it does seem reasonable to assume that schools where such conditions are present can selectively attract and retain people. But restructuring could lead to higher teacher morale without significantly changing teacher effectiveness; a host of studies of changes in working conditions in private industry demonstrate that job satisfication can increase without increases in productivity (Katz & Kahn, 1978).

In any case, the reasons restructuring could lead to student achievement are conditioned by the individual and collective competence levels of the teachers involved. Since competence is usually defined, both in current practice and research, as knowledge and behaviors that are correlated with student performance on standardized tests, we cannot assume that restructuring will lead to outcomes other than those conventionally assessed by such tests. How will restructuring figure significantly in teacher knowledge and teaching competence? Recent calls for restructuring do not typically incorporate resources and conditions that would allow teachers to learn more than their collective experiences in a given school could teach them.

If restructuring does lead to better teaching, the impact of that teaching will be affected by outside factors that influence student learning (outside the school). Thus far, restructuring proposals have not tried to change the relationships between schools and families. Indeed, some versions of restructuring would reduce the claims parents might make on schools just as the professionalization of law and medicine rendered clients and patients more dependent on lawyers and physicians.

Finally, the technical certainty of restructuring is undermined by some of the first wave proposals, especially those that prescribe student outcomes and teacher behaviors very explicitly. In those schools where Wave 1 reforms have been implemented, restructuring efforts are not likely to replace these newly established policies and procedures. Thus restructuring proposals will have to accommodate to constraints imposed by the first wave, and the Wave 2 reformers have not yet tackled this very difficult task.

The Missing Pieces: Families and Cognitive Development

I have argued that first wave reforms are both limited and limiting. While they may seem to raise the tide level, they lack the power to take our schools beyond mediocrity. Second wave reforms grapple with two more fundamental problems: enhancing mental capacity and remediating sources of learning difficulties among the disadvantaged and handicapped, on the one hand, and enhancing the quality of teaching on the other. Both of these second wave policies are essential, but neither goes far enough to solve the problems they seek to address if our goals are to significantly reduce the inequalities in student achievement and to enhance the intellectual capacity of the nation.

I have argued that neither of the two general strategies of the second wave come to grips with the role of families in educating our children. Further, I have argued that the proposed investment in teaching strategies probably cannot develop political consensus throughout the nation and takes for granted that changes in teacher quality and teaching conditions will markedly change the way learning is defined and facilitated in schools. These political and technical uncertainties are exacerbated by the almost total omission from teaching strategies of a role for parents, so that the family the social institution upon which the schools are most dependent politically and technically is not only without a new reason for engaging in efforts to improve schools but could also be estranged further.

Thus I conclude that the reform movement needs to be broadened and deepened in two major ways. First, families and schools need to be reconciled. Second, we must redefine the role of the teacher and change the way we conceptualize and facilitate learning.

Reconciling the Family and the School

For at least the last 50 years, those educators and social reformers who have seen schools as the mechanism through which individuals are prepared for social change have worried about the powerful influence the family has in preserving the status quo. This problem is confounded by the local and popular control of schools to a degree unmatched in any other industrialized nation. These worries have resulted, at best, in mixed signals to parents about their welcome in the schools (Berger, 1985).

Investment-in-children strategies have reflected a more pragmatic view of families. But, while most investment in children strategies recognize the family as part of the problem of increasing the cognitive capacity of babies and young children, the solutions proposed often take the current pathologies of "families" as given and limit efforts to strengthen the family's role in education to preschool and, perhaps, primary grades.

So, what can be done to reconcile the family and the school? I think there are two types of strategies that deserve consideration; programs and practices to involve parents in the education of their children and efforts to strengthen families. Obviously the first is easier and certainly less controversial than the second.

Involving parents in their children's education. Virtually all researchers who study student achievement agree that it is significantly related to the extent to which parents are actively involved in and otherwise provide support for their children's learning (Constable & Walberg, 1987). Programs aimed at enhancing student learning, which provide parents with the resources and responsiblity to assist their children, have a remarkable success recess rate (Hawley & Rosenholtz, 1984, Chap. 6). And, if there is one thing we should learn from studies of Japanese education, it is that parental involvement in children's education, more than any other factor, helps explain the high achievement of Japanese children (White, 1987; OERI, 1987).

So, if it is clear that parental involvement helps children learn, why isn't this a major part of the education reform agenda? There are many possible answers to this question, but two stand out: (a) many educators believe that many parents are not willing to devote much energy to their children's education, and (b) the demographics of dual-career couples and single-parent households and divorce, which complicate parental involvement in their children's education, are seen as inevitable and beyond remediation.

Despite the despair about parental involvement that seems to discourager elated reforms, there are things that can be done.

- Teacher initiatives can eliminate differences in parent involve ment between middle-class and lower-class parents and between one-parent and two-parent families (Epstein, 1986).
- Parents can learn how to help their children in preschool settings, in community organizations, and in churches, synagogues, and mosques.
- Electronic technology, such as computer-based telephone systems, can provide daily information to parents about student assignments.
- Homework assignments can provide opportunities for students to learn from parents and provide parents changes to be of help.
- Schools could be located in or near workplaces such an experiment is now underway in Miami to provide parents opportunities to be in schools, meet regularly with teachers, and talk with their children on the way to and from school and work.

No doubt there are other proposals that could involve parents more in their children's education. No one should expect things to change over night, even with imaginative programs. The process that currently estranges families from schools has been underway for decades (Berger, 1985), and the social forces rewarding parents for activities other than those related to their children's education and contributing to family instability are powerful. But it is hard to imagine that schools can be as effective without significant parent involvement as they can be when the interests and priorities of families and schools are congruent.

Strengthening families. This is not the place to assess the strength of American families. It does seem safe to say that the rate of divorce is too high, that the proportion of children born to unwed teenagers is appalling, and that too many marriages are characterized by verbal and physical abuse (Bergman, 1986). It also seems safe to say that, other things being equal, children whose parents divorce, who are born to unwed teenagers, and who witness or are the victims of abuse will not do as well in school as children who do not have such experiences.

If the health of families is important to children's learning, why isn't the health of families an important part of the school curriculum? One answer is that the moralistic character of family health has caused schools to stay away from the topic. Another answer is the feeling that we should be teaching academic subjects, not social behavior, in schools. Ironically, the increasing state control of curriculum may resolve some of the concerns that family-related curricula will become ways of teaching particular religious doctrines or offending the sensibilities of those who believe there should be no public posture about the value of strong families. There is nothing inherently nonacademic about the study of families. Their role in history, the impact of social change on families, ways of dealing with intrafamily stress, and the role of parenting in child development are all matters of serious scholarly inquiry. In any case, if schools are to transmit a nation's culture and build its capacity, neglecting curricula that might strengthen families probably predicts the future. Deciding what such curricula should look like could, in itself, be a first step toward reconciling families and schools.

Enhancing Cognitive Development

Let me recall two points made earlier. First, if school reform is to significantly alter the quality of life for individuals and help the nation solve its economic and social problems, it must go beyond improved performances on standardized tests and develop a capacity to learn, to be intellectually resilient, and to make better decisions in seeking to solve complex problems. Second, to assume that Wave 2 reforms in themselves will change how and what students learn because teachers are smarter or freer to pursue their own insights is a leap of faith that contradicts the central argument for the reforms that teaching is a complicated enterprise requiring special knowledge and competence that justifies calling it a profession.

Investment-in-children strategies do address cognitive development by seeking to prevent health-related limitations on intelligence and by seeking to enrich the environments and learning opportunities of younger children.

Paradoxically, strategies for invesring in teaching do not typically try to change the ways children learn. No doubt much of the problem is that the design of ways to foster cognitive development, like strategies for restructuring, have been speculative, and even the term itself lacked much precision. These difficulties persist, and are reflected both in sloppy conversation about what we are after and suggestions of unproven and unlikely solutions (like stand-alone courses on thinking, curricula based on right brain-left brain research, and teaching strategies based on convictions that learning styles are the causes rather than the products of learning).

In the last few years, however, research has emerged that could lead to preconceptions of the role of teachers and students in the teaching learning process (Resnick, 1987; Gardner, 1985). Carl Bereiter and Marlene Scardamelia (1987) have recently reviewed research on cognitive development and concluded that the linguistic and verbal reasoning abilities, literary standards and sophistication, and the moral values and precepts traditionally associated with elites are within the reach of most students. Other researchers have shown that new understandings of learning could dramatically enhance the capabilities of children to learn about science (Sherwood, Kinzer, Bransford, & Franks, 1987). But not if teachers structure learning opportunities as most teachers do. Bereiter and Scardamelia developed a composite model of teaching, the essential elements of which call for teachers to help students, on their own initiative, to activate prior knowledge, relate old knowledge to new in systematic and reflective ways, organize disparate pieces of information, and reach conclusions and assess those conclusions before settling on them. Bereiter and Scardamelia call this intentional learning. Students who engage in intentional learning not only are able to do the things outlined above, they are self-conscious about what they have learned in the process of learning and, even, why they learned what they did.

In fostering intentional learning, interests and motives are not treated as factors that influence what is learned; they are part of what is to be learned. Bereiter and Scardamelia (1987) suggest how Teacher C, their model teacher, would do this:

> Teacher C asks students themselves to recognize what is new and what is old information. Instead of asking questions of the students, Teacher C models the process of asking questions of the text or of oneself, and coaches the students in carrying out the modeled process. In writing, Teacher C makes use of external prompts, modeling, and peer cooperation to enable students to carry on their own Socratic dialogues, by means by which their knowledge is not only activated but reconsidered and evaluated in relation to what they are trying to write. Whereas Teacher B [our conventional model of an effective teacher] tries to minimize students' difficulties in comprehending and composing, Teacher C will sometimes assign reading or writing tasks that present special difficulties in order to provide occasions for teaching problem solving strategies. When difficulties arise they are treated as interesting phenomena for investigation, with the result that the students themselves become students of cognitive processes in reading and writing. (pp. 10-11)

Bereiter and Scardamelia argue that conventional modes of teaching focus on adaptive learning, the development of the competency to deal with the world as students experience it. This means that the students' immediate environments create the levels of cognitive demand they engage. Thus, as study after study shows, the students' social experiences (family, peers, community), rather than what is being taught in school or a particular educational program, accounts for the bulk of variations in student performance. It follows that the goal of significantly reducing the gap between the high and low-achieving youngsters, which I posited at the outset of this section, can best be achieved, perhaps only be achieved, if we change the way students learn. This, of course, will happen only if we change the way students are taught.

How can we foster "intentional learning"? A precondition is the restructuring of schools so that teachers have the opportunity and are motivated to create appropriate learning situations. As noted earlier, many of the first wave reforms assume that what children learn is more important than and independent from how they learn, so that good teaching is described in mechanistic terms and measured by student test performance that tell us little about student capacity for intentional learning.

It should be noted that the influence of first wave reforms lies not in the changes they brought about in teaching but in the fact that they reinforced and fine-tuned dominant practices that in turn were supported by the way schools are organized. Evidence for this conclusion can be found in the remarkable similarity of teaching styles and structure in American schools over time and across schools (Cuban, 1988; Goodlad, 1983).

There are three general ways to help teachers acquire greater competence and knowledge: preservice education, formal in-service training, and enriching opportunities for "incidental learning" in the context of teaching.

Proposals for reforming teacher education abound in both waves of reform, but they are without content (see, for example, proposals by the Holmes Group 1986, and the Carnegie Forum, 1986. That is, they focus on requirements for prospective teachers and the process of teacher education largely in terms of the number of courses taken and the mix of classroom and field or clinical experience. They give little attention to what is to be learned by teachers about teaching, learning, and schools.

In-service education and other formal opportunities for professional development generally receive low marks from teachers (Bacharach et al., 1986) and little attention from reformers. Presumably, teachers are to learn new ways to facilitate student learning on their own. Many restructuring proposals do create opportunities for learning from peers and from personal experiences. But this is not usually the focus of such proposals; thus the conditions that would best produce incidental learning receive little attention.

The idea that teachers will change the way they teach because we free them from bureaucratic constraints and provide them with opportunities to shape school policies and practices has a mystical quality to it. If we really want teachers to teach more effectively, we will have to teach them how. This means retraining teacher educators, creating induction processes (like so-called professional development centers), developing ways within school systems to enhance teacher learning, and using restructuring to empower teachers intellectually as well as politically and emotionally.

How technically certain is teaching that fosters intentional learning? There is considerable evidence that variations have worked in experimental situations, and the theoretical bases for this approach are supported by research. But like other promising educational innovations, we will not know whether they will work on a large scale until we try them on a large scale. That, in turn, will require considerably more research and development work and well-supported pilots.

Since we do not seem able to implement less ambitious improvements in teaching and learning, why set such high goals and invest in a somewhat utopian scenario? As I noted in the opening, the proposed investments in children and teaching that make up the second wave of the reform movement hold the promise of major changes in educational quality. But these improvements will not keep pace with our need and will fall short of our aspirations. while restructuring is needed to promote intentional learning, it is not sufficient. Most teachers do not intuitively teach with the sophistication outlined above. Achieving intentional learning capabilities for all children can move us within reach of the two goals outlined earlier. No other reform really does.

There is another, less altruistic reason for pursuing new approaches to teaching based on cognitive research. We have a better chance of achieving this high goal than do most other nations. For example, the Japanese government is seeking school reforms, hoping to achieve the outcomes that intentional learning produces students who are self-directed and active learners who can solve complex problems in creative ways (OERI, 1987, chap. 6). But Japanese schools and Japanese cultural values will have to change considerably more than ours will to achieve these results. On the other hand, there is no conceivable way that the first and second wave reforms now on the agenda will either (a) raise the level of mass education to Japanese levels when the measures are the acquisition of knowledge and basic skills or (b) socialize our young people to the values of perseverance and commitments to family and community that Japanese schools achieve. In short, our comparative educational advantage lies in upping the ante with respect to cognitive development.

Conclusion

I have tried to suggest the limitations of many of the proposals and the assumptions that compose the mainstream of both waves of the educational reform movement. I have argued that two important additional initiatives are essential if we wish to achieve greater equality of educational outcomes, significantly enhance capabilities to learn, and actively use such capabilities to solve problems. These complementary initiatives are to strengthen the role of parents in the education of their own children and to develop among teachers a capacity for new approaches to teaching that result in intentional learning.

Let me conclude by drawing attention to two ugly facts that represent the unposted undertow of the reform movement efforts and that significantly reduce both the political and technical certainty of almost all our reform efforts, especially those that seek to address fundamental and historic weakness in our schools. The first of these is the massive differences in social condition that set American students, as a whole, apart from the students of other industrialized societies. These differences can be ameliorated by quality education, but not much. The second fact that undermines efforts at educational improvement is the differences between our best and our worst schools. These differences are linked to differences in the resource base upon which schools can draw and, of course, to the problems that come from children living in poverty.

These realities have received remarkably little attention in the current debates over school reform (for an exception, see National

Coalition of advocates for Children, 1985). It is as though mentioning them would be an excuse not to undertake reform, or it would destroy the fragile consensus that keeps the reform efforts moving forward. But, unless we address these issues, the outcome of the reform movement is predictable: Differences in schools quality and social condition will increase, even if our worse schools improve somewhat and the effects of social disadvantages on children are somewhat ameliorated.

Addressing this undertow is beyond the reach of educational policy alone, of course. But the two pieces of the reform movement that I have argued are missing do speak directly to differences in the educational experience of children that are related to the inequalities we have trouble acknowledging.

3

Directions for Education Reform

"... An Act Of War"

To revisit the seminal work in the education reform movement of the 1980s—the 1983 report *A Nation at Risk*—is to experience a revelation. In retrospect, this opening salvo of the modern reform movement proves consistently prophetic, occasionally profound.

A Nation at Risk prefigures, in uncanny fashion, the host of issues that in time came to dominate our national dialogue on education reform. It presents, in tight and eloquent prose, a syllabus for a course on the future of American education, hinting at problems only dimly perceived in 1983 but soon deeply pursued and passionately debated.

A National At Risk touches all the bases: illiteracy, the decline in basic skills and graduation standards, the specter of a society deeply divided between a scientific elite and a lay citizenry bewildered by the rush of technological advances, the challenge of ethnic pluralism and the threat to the ideal of equity, the dropout syndrome and the teacher shortage, diluted curricula, banal textbooks, student discipline, teacher preparation, federal leadership, parental responsibility, and a portrait in miniature of a teaching profession under siege, undervalued, and underpaid.

A Nation at Risk is a remarkable document.

And yet, despite its scope, a single [paragraph dominates the whole. All else becomes a footnote. And what prevails is an analogy, bluntly militaristic, that defines education-decisively-as an *instrumental* value rather than an *intrinsic* value:

> If an unfriendly foreign power had attempted to impose on America the mediocre educational performance that exists today, we might well have viewed it as an act of war..... We have, in effect, been committing an act of unthinking, unilateral, educational disarmament.

It is only a bit hyperbolic to contend that these two sentences set the initial tone for the entire reform debate and dictated the direction of all but a few early reform initiatives. For these sentences defined the mission of education. The mission was decidedly utilitarian: Education was a weapon. This tenet was seldom challenged. It swiftly became the axiomatic foundation of education reform.

The mission of education was to serve the national interest. The destiny of American democracy, it was argued, demanded what revitalized education alone could deliver: technological prowess in the service of military security, economic rejuvenation in the service of reclaimed dominance within the international marketplace, the smooth social and political integration of new waves of immigrants in the service of national harmony.

Education was in the service now.

Not surprisingly, politicians volunteered for action. And, not surprisingly, what would later be termed the first wave of reform emanated not from the schoolhouse, but from the statehouse. Dictates from on high proliferated. An army of governors and state legislators swept into action. And their rallying cry—their battle cry—was "more": more tests for teachers, more credits for graduation, more hours in the school day, more days in the school year, more regimentation, more routinization.

Between 1983 and 1985, legislatures enacted more than 700 statutes stipulating what should be taught was and when, how and by whom it should be taught.

The reaction to this statutory mania not swift, but it was inevitable. And when the reaction arrived, it ushered in the second wave of reform.

The Changing Of The Guard

The second wave arose from the recognition that if education was to be an instrument for social and economic revitalization, the instrument ought to be wielded by educators, not legislators. Appearing before the annual meeting of the American Educational Research Association in April 1986, I presented the National Association's (NEA's) thesis that the time had come to reform movement:

> Every attempt at reform that dilutes the authority of the classroom teacher dilutes the quality of instruction in our nation's classrooms.
>
> Teachers cannot hope to prepare students for a world of perpetual flux if they themselves are condemned to static, externally imposed conceptions of effective pedagogy.
>
> Teachers cannot hope to prepare students for the information age if they themselves are condemned to organizational structures derived from the industrial age.
>
> Teachers cannot hope to ready students for responsibility within a participatory democracy if they themselves are condemned to an autocratic bureaucracy?

That was, in brief, the rhetoric of the second wave-its substance. By 1986, a growing body of research supported the contention that a rising tide of regulation, by wrenching decision-making authority away from teachers and principals, had produced a web of inefficiency. And in 1986, no fewer than five prestigious national reports condemned that inefficiency. The source of those reports were the Holmes Group, the Carnegie Commission, the National Governors' Association, the Education Commission of the States and the Association for Supervision and Curriculum Development.

Second-wave reform soon rested on a solid, research-based consensus. Scholars Theodore Sizer and Samuel Bacharach, each with a single statement, added exclamation points to the sentence that exiled first-wave reform. Said Sizer: "The decentralization of substantial authority to the persons closest to the students is essential." Said Bacharach: "Unless faculty are granted appropriate decision-making authority, education reform will remain a poorly disguised political sham-promising everything, delivering nothing."

During this second wave, professional recognition and professional autonomy for teachers became less distant, more realistic goals. The notion of top-down reform had been vanquished. Reform from the bottom up would now hold sway. Teacher empowerment would become at last more than an aspiration. NEA empowerment programs—the Mastery in Learning Project, Operation Rescue, and TABS (the Team Approach to Better Schools)-were launched in 1985 and 1986. All gave substance to the principle that effective reform must be designed and defined by teachers at the local level, working in concert with the local community.

The second-wave thrust was toward reform efforts that would bring together teachers, principals, superintendents, school board members, parents, and business and community leaders in a culture of cooperation. The local school site would be the focus of reform, and reform initiatives would be tailored to local needs.

But exiles return. More precisely: what remained from first-wave reform was the emphasis on education as an instrumental rather than an intrinsic value. Most reforms, even the most creatively crafted, continued to be justified purely on the grounds of national interest. Economic imperatives took the place of legislative mandates. This emphasis,t his economic utilitarianism, generated the third wave of reform. Its parentage could be traced, not to the second, but to the first wave of reform. The "top", this time more economic than political, was again driving the reform agenda.

It was at this point that educators recognized the need to forge a broader agenda—an agenda that defined education as *both* an instrumental *and* an intrinsic value.

The Economic Battleground

In the United States today, the prevailing assumption remains that all will be right with our nation if only education is so reformed that it is guided exclusively by the twin goals of catching the Japanese economically and matching the Soviets militarily. These goals, however, cannot in themselves prepare today's students for the world they will inherit tomorrow. For that world—the "global village"-will demand zealous compassion as much as competitive zeal. Just as surely, it will demand emotional resiliency, mental, agility, moral stamina, and the creative savvy to improvise successfully in the face of unrelenting change and unforeseen challenges. These virtues represent the *intrinsic* values of education that, until, now, the reform debate has too frequently neglected.

How do we explain this flaw? And how do we prevent this flaw from becoming fatal? We might start by examining the vocabulary that now dominates discussions of education. We are told with increasing regularity that knowledge is a *commodity* education an *industry* learning an *asset,* research an *enterprise.* Talk of intellectual *capital* is commonplace. A stubborn consensus holds that the business of education is business.

There is, of course, no denying that the business community and the education community must work together more closely and more cooperatively. Indeed, the corporate community may be public education's most valuableally. But when the language of commerce so thoroughly saturates discourse on education, something is amiss. Is a mercantile mentality compatible with the traditional missions of public education? Can an education that is *both* an *Instrumental value* in the service of national interests *and* a *noninstrumental, nonutilitarian value* that elevates character and educates "the whole child" be forged on the anvil of economic imperatives?

Not likely.

Harvard University economist Robert Reich, author of the landmark treatise *Education and the Next Economy,* which addresses precisely the issue of how to make education a more powerful *economic instrument* nonetheless takes care to issue a stern caveat:

> By focusing on education and the next economy, I do not mean to suggest that education's only, or most important, purpose is economic. To the contrary: A truly educated person is motivated by, and can find satisfaction in, a wide array of things that are not traded in markets or that cost very little. A just and democratic society depends on a citizenry educated in civic responsibility rather than in economic aggrandizement.

Reich goes on to fortify his position by quoting with approval the eloquent statement Horace Mann issued to the Boston Board of Education in 1842. Defending the cause of public education. Mann ended his address by saying.

> [H]owever deserving of attention may be the *economical* view of the subject which I have endeavored to present, yet it is one that dwindles into insignificance when compared to those loftier and more sacred attributes of the cause.

None of this is to deny that education is the engine that drive our economic. *But it does not follow that our economy ought to be the engine that drives education.* The simple fact—the incontrovertible fact—is that we will do a disservice to students if we offer them no more than a curriculum designed to advance economic goals or serve utilitarian objectives.

During the past two decades, we have seen the dangers of education designed to serve narrow, provincial priorities—priorities defined by the crisis of the hour. We have also seen the results of this subservience: graduates who are skilled but uneducated, short on creativity, incapable of synthesizing new information. Graduates who draw a blank when asked what images come to mind when they hear the words Soweto and Gdansk, Managua and Phnom Penh, Hiroshima and Auschwitz. Graduates who (the greatest irony of all) are condemned to routinized, dead-end jobs that deprive them of pride and drive them toward debt.

These students are ill prepared for both the world we know and the world we know is approaching. In this, there is no surprise. The obsolete curriculum they were offered—this subservient curriculum-advances *neither* the ethical *nor* the economic agendas our nation embraces.

Education—even if defined only as an instrument to advance national goals-conquers ignorance. A more balanced education—education free from subservience and forged with at least one eye to its intrinsic value—has the potential to conquer intellectual myopia. The education that emerges from this broader agenda will not bow to parochial interests.

Those parochial interests will, of course, persist—and rightly so. Parents may seek an education that offers their children a route to fortune or fame. Corporate executives may seek an education that prepares their future employees to increase corporate earnings. Governments may seek an education that prepares students for active and responsible citizenship. These respective agendas are beyond reproach, and educators must both respect these agenda and remain responsive to them. At the same time, we can never allow a single goal to define our mission.

Educators must accept the premise that the mission of education is of necessity defined by a coherent vision of the kind of world we wish our children to inherit. More important still, it is defined by a vision of the values that will prepare students to cope, indeed to flourish, in that new world.

What now seems clear, as the intellectually demanding and precariously balanced world of the twenty-first century comes into view, is that the mission of education must not be to train people to *serve* the purposes of others, but to develop their capacity to *question* the purposes of others. We must equip students with stupidity detectors. We must bolster their will seek wisdom. We must enable them to think complexly and creatively, to act responsibly, and —when necessary—to act selflessly. We must convince then that the gross national product is not a measure of our worth as a people.

The fourth wave of reform will demand a return to schools that are organized to facilitate bottom-up reform. The goals of education-defined as both an instrumental and an intrinsic value—must become less parochial, more expansive, more animated by good, will less determined by economic forces.

Peace

The curricula that will emerge from fourth-wave reform will, because forged at the local level, exhibit no uniformity. But they will, if reform does indeed become less wed to instrumentalist goals, share a common feature. Specifically our curricula—designed to prepare students for a radically pluralistic, "shrunken" world—will be less deeply rooted in the classics of Western civilization. The classics will not be forsaken nor traditional curricula jettisoned. But those curricula will be expanded, supplemented, stretched.

We can, of course, learn much—and much of value—from the giants of the classical tradition. Pythagoras, to cit only one example, has more than a few lessons for fourth-wave reforms. For Pythagoras might be characterized as a radical interdisciplinarian. It was he who insisted that the most intimate of all disciplines are mathematics..... and music.

The strict back-to-basic advocates might want to give this puzzle some thought. For these advocates, in the interest of producing a citizenry (more precisely, a work force) that can read and count, all too often define the arts—and music in particular—as inadequately instrumental, as educational frills. This characterization is unacceptable to anyone who believes that education must serve personal human needs at least as much as serves national economic goals.

Music is among the keys that offers us access to the souls of civilizations past and civilizations still in the making. It is the language of the emotions. Not raw emotion, but emotion rendered articulate, emotion corralled by intellect. Anyone who understands the difference between cacophony and a symphony has begun to understand the meaning of civilization—the meaning of the quest to wrench order from chaos.

Is there utility in that understanding? Very likely. Is there intrinsic value? Most assuredly. Similar statements could be made about sculpture and painting, literature and dance, foreign languages and geography. These disciplines are—to borrow the fashionable cliche—windows of opportunity. Those windows must remain open, for through them flows the air that awakens and sustains the understanding that fosters self-understanding.

But a balanced curriculum demands still more. Fourth-wave education must have both instrumental and intrinsic value, must help the United States meet both economic and moral imperatives. To that end, that education must neglect neither artistic nor scientific content.

Today, more than ever before, a well-trained cadre of scientists is essential if our global village is to be free from pestilece, fee from hunger, free from fear. Acquired immune deficiency syndrome, to invoke the obvious example, has taught us that viruses do not respect national boundaries and do not discriminate on the basis of race, gender, or ethnicity. Nor should science. Any scientific discovery that can improve the lot of the human family belongs to that family. This fact is decisive. It points to the need for an education that serves our *national* interest even as it awakens us to the *common* interests we share with all nations and all peoples. Our highest aspirations cannot be achieved and our most sublime intentions cannot find expression without an education in which instrumental and intrinsic values intersect.

Perhaps no ideal conveys this lesson more powerfully than the ideal of peace, the kind of peace President Kennedy described—"peace that enables men and nations to grow and to hope and to build a better life *for their children*—not merely peace for Americans, but peace for all men and women ..... not merely peace in our time, but peace for all time" [emphasis added]. With the introduction of this issue, the dichotomy that has informed this chapter can no longer be sustained. Peace is an instrumental value, and peace is an intrinsic value. The issue of peace brings into focus the most compelling argument for an education defined by an intersection of values, values that are economic, political, social, ethical, national—and *transnational.*

The goal of fourth-wave reform is no longer obscure. That goal is an education that prepares tomorrow's adults to meet economic imperatives as well as ethical imperatives, that prepares them not early for a life of work but for a life of worth, that steels their resolve to exhibit fidelity not only to the most sacred principles that unite the American family, but to principles that can bring harmony to the human family.

The fourth wave of education reform has the potential to so transform the educational landscape that in years hence, the question "Is education an instrumental value or an intrinsic value?" will be unintelligible. This either/or question will be unintelligible because the answer- the one right answer—will be "Yes".

If that happens-*when* that happens—we will have fulfilled the promise of American education. We will have met the mandates of *A Nation at Risk* without yielding to the one-dimensional, instrumentalist ideology of *A Nation at Risk*. That's the best of both worlds. That's the promise-and the challenge—of fourth-wave education reform.

4

A Career in the Classroom

The teaching career has recently been the subject of considerable public policy discussion, focused primarily upon (1) demographic shifts affecting teacher supply and demand (Guthrie, 1987; Cagampang, Guthrie, & Kirst, 1986; Hodgkinson, 1985); (2) the academic background and preparation of K-12 classroom teachers (Lanier & Little, 1986; Schlechty, 1985); and (3) analysis of the teacher's role, salary, working conditions, and opportunities for career advancement (Boyer, 1988; Odden, 1987).

The purpose of this analysis is to describe two of the public policy issues emerging in this discussion and their implications for future developments. These particular issues arose in the course of a year-long seminar conducted in 1987-1988 by the California State Department of Education, in cooperation with the Commission on Teacher Credentialing and a group of faculty members in the Graduate School of Education, Stanford University. Over 200 teachers, administrators, college and university faculty, and other educators participated in the deliberation. In brief, the central issues discussed were as follows:

- New teacher assessment and support programs should be viewed as part of the larger agenda to restructure the teaching occupation. Otherwise, they run the risk of becoming an isolated categorical initiative.

- In the current political climate, staff development assistance for new teachers in the form of additional resources will be provided only in exchange for greater accountability, defined at the induction level as candidate-based demonstrations of competence for teaching as part of a professional licensure decision. We currently know much more about the crucial elements for supporting new teachers than about how to mount the comprehensive formative and summative assessments implied by proposals to move to a candidate-based credentialing system (California State Department of Education, in press).

The Resource—Accountability Exchange

Teacher licensure reform and induction needs were embedded in many of the commissioned reports calling for the restructuring of the teaching occupation (e.g., the Carnegie, Homes, American Association of Colleges of Teacher Education (AACTE), American Federation of Teachers (AFT), National Education Association (NEA), and California Commission on the Teaching Profession reports). Calls to professionalize the occupation are in response to the historic definition of the teaching career path as organized around labor, art, and craft models (Kerchner & Mitchell, 1988). These concerns are reflected in the working conditions of many teachers, where bargained agreements view teaching primarily as a technical skill and where a majority of teachers still do not participate in central professional activities, including staff selection, budgeting, professional development, evaluation, and a host of student standards and policy issues (Boyer, 1988).

The lack of support for new teachers, the availability of more lucrative and higher status jobs elsewhere, and the absence of any individually based accountability mechanism for ensuring teacher mastery of knowledge and skills all weaken teaching's claim to be a profession and encourage exit from the occupation and rapid turnover. This is particularly problematic in the sunbelt states of the Southeast and Southwest, where there is an increasing demand for classroom teachers (Grissmer & Kirby, 1987). The Policy Analysis for California Education (PACE) research group predicts that the state will need between 77,300 and 85,000 additional K-12 teachers by 1989-

90 and between 159,700 and 183,400 by 1994-1995 to allow for both enrollment growth and attrition (Guthrie & Kirst, 1988.).

New teacher induction programs are particularly appropriate to help address the developmental needs of new teachers. Historically we have assumed that a teacher's education is largely complete once the initial hurdle of licensure has been cleared. This contrasts with other professions, such as nursing, accounting, and law, where an individual's relative newness in the profession is recognized, and new professionals receive the supervision of more experienced peers, take responsibility for fewer clients, and are expected to grow into their role. By contrast, we frequently give our newest teachers the same teaching load as their more experienced colleagues, with as many students and extracurricular assignments as are given to the ten-year veteran. In fact, research indicates that the newest teachers often have the toughest assignments, in the worst classrooms, with inadequate curriculum materials and supplies, and little opportunity either to vent their frustrations or to learn from their peers (McLaughlin, 1986).

Support services for novice teachers serve simultaneously as continued training for the individual, as an institutional service to help schools organizationally receive new teachers, and as a safeguard for the public. Such programs typically include opportunities for participants to be supervised in their initial teaching role, to get feedback on their teaching strengths and weaknesses, and increasingly to inform the state's decision to grant them a full professional license. Taxpayers and policymakers are linking resources for induction programs to stronger measures of teacher accountability. Candidate-based assessment for licensure was proposed in a number of the commissioned reports and featured in our seminar discussions as one approach to strengthening the teaching occupation and putting it more on a par with other professions that require prospective practitioners to demonstrate knowledge and the ability to use knowledge in performance settings as a prerequisite for earning a license.

Candidate-based assessment means that prospective practitioners are individually tested for licesure; if deficient, they are either given additional assistance to help them along the route to full professional status or are counseled out of the occupation. This contrasts with a *program approval* approach to licensure, which assumes that program graduates have mastered the requisite professional knowledge if the preparation program itself has been "approved." In a candidate-based approach, novices are asked instead to demonstrate their knowledge and skill directly on some form of assessment, typically a range of measures that are designed to document knowledge and skill in teaching and serve either formative or summative purposes, or both. The formation component is particularly important in teaching, where a growing body of research literature documents the differences in teaching knowledge held by expert and novice teachers in their own subject area (Berliner, 1988; Leinhardt & Greeno, 1986; Pecheone, Garon, Forgione, & Abeles, 1988).

A number of states, including California, have connected the desire to move to a candidate-based assessment system with a commitment to provide a support system for beginning teachers. Such a system constitutes an exchange relationship that reflects the dual policy priorities of improving teacher preparation, compensation, and working conditions while also increasing teacher accountability. Salaries constitute the largest part of school budgets, and in the current fiscal climate state legislatures are increasingly reluctant to augment teacher salaries without concomitant demonstrations of competence.

These parallel efforts, then—one to provide a range of services for new teachers during their early, induction years and the other to link the award of the professional teaching credential to successful practice during induction- are being implemented in at least 11 states (Goertz, 1986). More are likely to follow as teachers seeking competitive salaries lobby in state legislatures committed to more accountability in return for greater resources.

Prototype Programs to Support New Teachers

Several state-supported programs underway in California are providing evidence of the forms new-teacher support can take and the ways a candidate-based assessment system might inform teacher licensure. The New Teacher Retention Project in Inner City Schools is sponsored by the California State University chancellor's office and the state department of education, working with San Diego State University and the San Deigo Unified School District, and with Hayward State University and the Oakland Unified School District. This pilot program is intended to increase the retention of new inner-city classroom teachers. although the program is relatively small, early data suggest that new teachers in these settings are staying in the profession.

In a second initiative, 768 first- and second-year teachers are participating in an evaluation study of new-teacher assessment and support. Under the direction of the state education and teacher licensing departments, 15 pilot programs are being implemented to identify the kinds of specific state policies needed to ensure the retention and effectiveness of new teachers. The 15 funded projects involve individual school districts working alone; districts sharing governance with colleges, universities, and teachers' organizations; and large consortia composed of school districts, country offices of education, and institutions of higher education. An assessment component is analyzing the role of formative and summative assessments of new teachers in improving their initial teaching performance, and whether and how such assessments should be used as one requirement for state certification. An evaluation will document the success of the program in increasing teacher retention, effectiveness, satisfaction, collegiality, and commitment to the profession.

A number of other initiatives, sponsored by colleges, universities, and large school districts around California already support new teachers through site-level programs, telecommunications, college and university seminars, and staff development programs targeted specifically to the needs of the new teachers. The seminar series identified a number of elements crucial to the success of these programs and to the reform of teacher credentialing practices. Each of these areas is summarized next.

1. *The design of a new teacher support program needs to be*

built around the defined purposes of the program and involve those most directly affected—teachers, administrators, and college and university faculty. Any of the following purposes might be encouraged in a program for new teachers, including: orientation to district and school, psychological support, teaching assistance, expansion of subject matter and pedagogical skills, evaluation for staff development or employment, identification with the teaching profession, and increased professional colleagueship (Wise et al., 1987). where purposes are in part specified (e.g., by legislation), opportunity needs to be given for local elaboration to reflect local priorities, existing support services, and unique features of the local environment.

2. *Connections to other initiatives, including teacher recruitment, selection, staff development, teacher evaluation and school improvement need to be establishments, preferably early in the design, to increase the chances for later institutionalization.* Even if the new-teacher support program is intended only to help new teachers during the initial survival stage, it is important that the people and perspectives of those involved in other efforts be incorporated in the design to promote a sense of ownership and the likelihood of later institutionalization.

3. *Teachers should be selected for the support program on the basis of program purposes, design, and new teachers needs.* All teachers working in new situations can benefit from induction support, but a new-teacher support program cannot be everything to all people. Experience suggests that when different kinds of new teachers are included in a support program, consideration should be given to modifying the program content, duration, and level of support and supervision to reflect prior teaching experience, levels of teaching proficiency, and continuing need for the support.

4. *A variety of individuals from different organizations are qualified to work with new teachers, although they need training for the role.* Experienced teachers, mentors, college faculty, and school and district administrators are likely candidates to provide support for new teachers. In particular, school principals

have a pivotal role in setting the tone for new teacher support, both in the assignments given new teachers and in providing resources for staff development and school improvement. Many of them will have taught elementary and/or secondary school themselves. However, they will likely need orientation and training for their support roles—training that reflects adult learning needs. Adults learn best when they are presented with meaningful experiences in the course of real work, when training builds upon those experiences and anticipates that they will be differentially motivated by particular learning experiences (Krupp, 1987).

5. *Support services for new teachers are likely to be variants on three dominant approaches. These are: personal support, professional consulting, and seminars and coursework.* Regardless of the approach or provider (typically a district or post-secondary institution), support systems should be designed to provide assistance that is context-specific and, as much as possible, based on the individual needs of the new teachers.

Initially, most new teachers will want to be paired with an experienced teacher in their own building, preferably in their subject area or grade level, to help with the first difficult weeks. Over time, teacher needs will change, and local programs need to be designed to accommodate different teacher learning needs. At differential rates, new teachers will need opportunities to learn more about their subject matter and how to teach it, how students learn and how instruction should be modified to reflect individual differences, the norms of schools as organizations, and their own roles as members of the teaching occupation.

Induction into the profession implies the development of a set of values and mores about good teaching. To develop these norms, new teachers and their more experienced colleagues need opportunities to talk about teaching, share their individual conceptions of teaching, and build understanding and commitment to the profession.

The relationship between new teachers and their support personnel is a key variable in the success of the new teacher and the support program (Ward, 1988). If the support is provided by other teachers, new teachers and their support partners need to be in close proximity. Opportunities need to be provided for new teachers to observe both one another and their more experienced colleagues. If the support is provided by the university, faculty must be able to work at the new teacher's school site on a regular basis.

The forms of support should match the anticipated goals. This means that the program should be designed toward specific outcomes. Thus, although a before-school orientation is useful, it is unlikely to develop new knowledge and skill unless the orientation sessions are part of an ongoing staff development program. Similarly, if collegiality is a goal of the new teacher support system, time and opportunity must be provided for teachers to work together (McDonald, 1980).

6. *Seminars and college and university coursework for new teachers needs to be practical.* Higher education plays an important role in new-teacher support and can be crucial in helping new teachers make the transition from student / student teacher to classroom teacher of record and teaching professional. The demands of the new classroom, however, make it important that coursework offered for teachers during their first year be extremely practical. Where coursework is theoretical, it needs to be offered either during a second year or over a two-year period, because first-year teachers are simply attending to too many other issues at the outset of their career (Ward, 1988).

7. *Time and compensation need to be provided for new teachers and their support personnel to work together.* Regardless of the design, new-teacher support programs require resources. Curricular, instructional, and man-agreement skills are developed through opportunities to practice them with more experienced others—mentors, faculty, and school administrators. Both the experienced teacher and the novice need time for this work, and the time needs to be recognized. There are a variety of ways to provide this recognition, including salary compensation, released time, reduced teaching loads, reduced additional responsibilities, ceremonies of recognition, and other rewards. A compensation package that new teachers and other faulty regard as meaningful should be collaboratively developed.

One caution about released time: A little goes a long way. Both evaluation data and informal reports from the New Teacher Retention Project in Inner City Schools document that neither new teachers nor their administrators want large amounts of released time (Money, 1988). An initial requirement for 20 percent released time has been relaxed in favor of more flexible scheduling of time for new teaches to work with faculty and mentors. Released time is expensive; new teachers are burdened when they are required to prepare extensive lesson plans; they don't want to be out of their own classrooms for extended periods; and substitutes are difficult to find. (During 1988-1989, we are experimenting with 5 to 20 days of released time per year in various settings.)

8. *A formative assessment component is a critical part of any teacher support program and may be linked to teacher evaluation. The formative assessment* side of a teacher support program is crucial. Depending on the program's purposes, formative assessment may be used to design individual or staff development plans for general program revision. The success of the formative component depends in large part on the extent to which teachers and their advisors trust its accuracy, fairness, and utility. Some of the better systems provide frequent feedback to new teachers about their teaching, opportunities for novices to learn new subject matter and practice new instructional strategies, assessments of teaching performance with diverse student groups, and resources for individualized professional development programs tied to school improvement activities.

Some districts may elect to tie formative assessment to teacher evaluation and employment decisions. Poway, California, has such a system. There is considerable debate about whether the same individual can both formatively and summatively assess a new teacher. Regardless of who conducts the evaluation, the evaluation system itself needs to be developed collaboratively with teachers, related directly to identified instructional goals, and linked to staff development (McLaughin & Pfeiffer, 1988). Those who are evaluating the new teacher need to be trained for that role, and the criteria on which the new teacher is to be evaluated need to be collaboratively defined. As one personnel director put it, "A teacher evaluation system should provide no surprises."

9. *Monetary and human resources, site leadership, and flexibility in program design are essential for implementation and a key to institutionalizing a new-teacher support system.* An overwhelming majority of respondents in a study of new-teacher support programs in the Southeast reported insufficient funding as the major program weakness. Respondents also cited inadequate compensation for mentors, faculty, and university staff working on new-teacher induction (Hawk & Robards, 1987). Educational systems need to plan and budget for new-teacher induction, not assume that it can be supported without resources. Nevertheless, a local system to recognize and support the developmental status of the new teacher need not be costly. Pilot programs with existing mentor teachers, telephone hotlines to answer personal and professional questions, and before-school orientations can provide important services for new teachers and set the stage for a larger initiative.

At the same time, new-teacher support must be an explicit initiative if it is to be successful. Site administrative support is key here, as is design flexibility, so the program can be refined over time.

10. *The development of support systems for new teachers needs to be encouraged not as separate categorical programs but as part of a local staff development system.* Ironically, to define its goals and develop a constituency, an educational initiative is most frequently defined as a *program.* In the process, the program takes on a life of its own, develops a categorical constituency, and then is only reluctantly institutionalized into the system. (Witness the uneasy incorporation of special-population strategies into the mainstream of the educational program.) New teachers are just entering the system, and whatever efforts we support on their behalf need to help them become part of the whole enterprise, rather than a categorical class.

Staff development also has a larger mission than simply improving the individual new teacher's skills. The findings of the

CPEC State Staff Development Policy Study illuminate the need for staff development to be broadened from the categorical definitions of in-service courses and after school seminars to become part of the everyday fabric of teachers' work on curriculum and instruction (Little & Geritz, 1987).

Staff development is also an important vehicle for encouraging teacher professionalism. As noted by Kanthak and Mitchell (1988),

> The goals of individual teacher accountability and the creation of professional standards throughout the occupation remain strong, but they are now balanced by a new set of goals. Direct investment in teacher staff development over the last three decades has been stimulated by the need to reform school programs and curricular structures, not simply to improve the performance of individual teachers. Professionalism means accepting responsibilities for leadership with the school and district as well as competence in the classroom.

The Difficulties and Potentials of A New-Teacher Assessment System

Increased professional accountability within a more collegial, professional environment is the other side of the teacher support equation. Key to the development of proposals for new teacher support are parallel calls to make teacher preparation and assessments for the credential more rigorous.

Assessment for licensure during a teacher induction program is a complex matter. The high-stakes nature of licensure assessment requires that strict standards of equity and fairness be observed and that the teaching context not condition performance (Wise et al., 1987). Licensure is a public protection, a quality control assurance that guarantees the public that an individual meets minimal expectations for performing in an occupation. Although data can and should be drawn from naturalistic settings (as in a medical or architectural residency), licensure requirements need to include a combination of state standardized measures and applied performance tests, along with observational data and recommendations from individuals who work with the new teacher (Darling-Hammond & Wise, 1985).

Standardized tests have historically been used in teacher licensure because of their statistical ability to document levels of psychometric validity and reliability and their ease of administration. We have created a mystique surrounding many tests of basic skills because we have the capacity to measure them. However, a central component of efforts to define a more comprehensive candidate-based assessment process is recognition that individual knowledge, skills, attributes, and abilities need to be demonstrated through performance in teaching, in addition to, or in lieu of, completion of coursework or standardized pencil-and-paper tests.

Building such a system is difficult. Although we think we know what good teaching looks like, we do not have a consensus on the complexity of its measurement. How would such a system be organized? First and foremost, it would have both formative and summative components, junctures at which individuals would receive information about their performance and be encouraged either to continue with professional development or to consider an alternative career. Second, a comprehensive teacher assessment system would have multiple measures, rather than one or two tests on which individuals must achieve a designated passing score in order to teach. Third, such a system would inform both teacher education and the credentialing process (Wise et al., 1987).

The California New Teacher Project is examining these issues, many of which are being analyzed in evaluation and assessment work being conducted by the Southwest Regional Educational Laboratory (SWRL) and the Far West Regional Educational Laboratory (FWL). Important work is also being done in Minnesota by the Rand group, as well as by the Connecticut State Department of Education, the states participating in the Southern Regional Educational Board consortium, and the Interstate New Teacher Assessment and Support Consortium. The challenges of creating a valid and reliable assessment system for licensing beginning teachers are many, particularly when the goal is to ensure that licensed teachers have not only a grasp of the subject matter they will teach, but also the knowledge and skill required to teach effectively (Shulman, 1988; Millman, 1988).

Other critical issues that must be addressed in a teacher assessment system include the need to:

- Define the knowledge, skill, and expectations of documenting teaching demonstration in straightforward yet nontrivial ways.
- Provide candidates with adequate opportunities to master the knowledge and skills on the measures prior to licensure assessment.
- Ensure that the assessments themselves do not differentially affect one group of candidates over another.
- Require a combination of measures—for example, site-based, naturalistic observations of teaching along with standardized measures of knowledge and simulations of ability to teach.
- Include a diagnostic component to inform staff development decisions (California State Department of Education, in press).

We can expect individual states to take different approaches to candidate-based assessment for teacher licensure. Reflecting different environments, curricula, instructional priorities, and values in teaching, approaches to licensure assessment will necessarily differ. For instance, in states of any size, performance assessments would necessarily have to be conducted locally because of the cost. Opinion is divided about whether the individuals who provide the staff development support for new teachers can, in an unbiased fashion, also participate in their summative evaluation (Griffin & Millies, 1987). In states like Oklahoma, the new teacher is supported and evaluated by the same people; in other settings, the support and assessment components are kept strictly separate. The current evaluation study in California is experimenting with both approaches. Regardless of who conducts the assessment, states should anticipate an increased cost if performance assessments are to be included: States currently conducting on-site assessments estimate the costs at $500 to $2,600 per teacher (Brooks, 1987).

Summary

Do new teachers need special staff development and assessment assistance during their first year or early years in teaching? If so, what kinds of assistance work best for what kinds of individuals in what kinds of settings? Can such assistance have an impact on teacher retention, effectiveness, satisfaction, professionalism, and commitment to staff development? Does it truly inform the credentialing process? Should it? How much should new-teacher assessment and support reasonably cost? Who much should new-teacher assessment and support reasonably cost? Who should pay?

These are some of the central questions being asked and answered in evaluations of teacher induction programs around the United States. Extant research suggests that new teachers teach better if they are provided with the resources to teach fewer students; have access to various curricular, instructional, and management resources; and have opportunities to work with one another and with experienced teacher role models (Fox & Singletary, 1986; Schlechty, 1985; Ward, 1988). But should states pay for these services? Are there real benefits of broadening the scope of the licensure assessment, so we are not relying solely on a single standardized measure?

These questions do not lend themselves well to quick answers, as it will take time to track new teacher retention, satisfactions, effectiveness, and commitment to the career. The development of the performance assessments will also be costly and time-consuming as we ensure that they measure performance equitably, without penalizing some candidates. Nevertheless, both the support and the assessment components in these ventures hold real promise. The support components recognize that teachers, like other professionals, need to grow into their role. The assessment components reflect another feature of professionalism self-monitoring of those who practice the profession. Taken together, new teacher support and assessment can make a real contribution to the development of the profession as a whole. They can do so, however, only if given time and resources to develop, and if the other elements of professionalism decision-making discretion, competitive compensation, and career opportunity—are also advanced.

5

Creative Teaching

Hear Is A Puzzle. In almost every recent account of "good" or "successful" or "effective" schools, the observer or analyst eventually admits that whatever else is going on, the quality of teaching is unremarkable. Drop-out rates may be down, test scores up, kids, teachers, and parents satisfied, but the teaching itself most often appears flat, unimaginative, and uniform, There are exceptions to be sure, but whether the observer is Sara Lightfoot (1983), Joan Lipsitz (1984), Theodore Sizer (1984), or Michael Rutter et al. (1979), there comes a point when each reluctantly comments on the teaching itself. The schools they visit may be good, the principals dynamic, the curriculums rich, the culture strong, the expectations high but.....

But the teaching does not stand out.

Large-scale studies of schooling tend to confirm the impressions of these and other observers. John Goodlad's 1984 study, for example, contains dispiriting evidence drawn from a large sample of schools. Both Goodlad and Kenneth Sirotnik (1983) found at elementary and secondary levels, and with little variation across or within schools that,

* teachers "outtalk" students by a 3:1 ratio;
* teachers provide little corrective feedback to students;
* teachers devote little time to questioning of any sort and almost no time to open questions that call for complex cognitive and emotional responses;
* whole-class instruction predominates, with almost no independent smallgroup, or cooperative work by students;

* emotions rarely appear in classrooms;

* there is little praise, enthusiasm, or intensity of any sort. Classrooms are emotionally neutral, affectless places.

Summarizing this data, Sirotnik Writes,

> Consider again the model classroom picture presented here: a lot of teacher talk and a lot of student listening, unless .students are responding to teachers' questions or working on written assignments; almost invariable.closed an factual questions; little corrective feedback and no guidance; and predominantly total class instructional configurations and traditional activities all in a virtually affectless environment. It is but a short inferential leap to suggest that we are implicitly teaching dependence upon authority; linear thinking; social apathy; passive involvement, and hand-off learning. This so-called "hidden curriculum" is disturbingly apparent. (p.29)

Now place this description next to an observation: The "effective schools" research from which factors for school management are derived is entirely silent on the question of teaching. The emphasis is on "instructional leadership" high expectations, clear objectives, test-curriculum alignment, coordination of instruction, and the like. These are all crucially important matters, but I want tc point out that there is no conception within this literature of what constitutes good teaching or good learning.

Here, then, is our situation. We identify successful schools within which much teaching is pedestrian and uninspired. And we create a management literature on schooling that leaves out the core activity of the organization. Does this strike anyone as peculiar?

This tendency has a parallel within the literature on teaching itself. There the emphasis rests on classroom management and on generic teaching skills that tend to ignore subject matter and responsiveness to individual students. What seems peculiar from one angle, however, is quite understandable from another. These approaches serve well the needs and interests of school administrators and school teachers respectively. Both have strong needs for predictability and control in their work environments.

Teachers daily confront dozens of fractious students all of whom may not be fascinated with the school curriculum. The first and continuing imperative of teaching is to establish and maintain an orderly classroom to set up rules and routines that support predictable patterns of behavior. Only within an orderly environment can teaching proceed. The enemy is disruption, and the precious resource is time. Teachers seize on methods that increase their efficiency in managing students in large groups.

School principals likewise are under pressure to produce. They are responsible for aggregate results—test scores, drop-out rates, advanced placement, college attendance, and school climate. They must ensure that instruction is coordinated across grade levels and that what is tested corresponds to what is taught. But their span of control is long, and they are generalists managing the work of specialists. They have neither the time nor the expertise to monitor the work of individual teachers. They require broad and efficient control strategies to manage the work of the organization. The effective schools research provides a cognitive map of schooling that directs attention to a manageable set of factors. Not surprisingly, then, the most popular and prevalent approaches to school improvement help solve the most pressing problems faced by teachers and administrators.

Is there a problem here? If these approaches result in orderly classrooms and higher test scores, do we care what the teaching looks like? I want to make the case that the quality of teaching does matter, that the evidence of a uniform, beige pedagogy is worrisome, and that approaches to school management that ignore teaching quality are inadequate.

My argument concerns the nature of means and ends in education, the relation of teaching to learning. The twin claims are that, in practice,

* we cannot justify teaching solely on the basis of its outcomes; but,
* we cannot justify teaching absent *some* evidence that it has produced a desirable outcome.

These assertions have significance for how we evaluate

teaching, how we manage schools, and how we seek to improve them. But each claim first requires some defense.

Consider the case of a teacher or a school principal who seeks credit for improvements on test scores or other educational outcome indicators. Without the opportunity to judge the means used, we cannot give a whole-hearted endorsement. Any educational acts, methods, or systems have multiple consequences for students; not all of them can be measured simply and accurately. Teachers must consider the social effects of their instructional strategies, must balance what is good for the individual with what is necessary in the group, must provide opportunities to acquire basic skills, cultural literacy, *and* higher-order thinking, must attend to the emotional lives of students, and must create a learning community that teaches civic virtues—tolearnce, fairness, justice, and empathy.

Teaching is a complex activity that requires constant decision making about means and ends. Judging teaching largely on one or two outcomes ignores too much of to what ends teachers must attend, while avoiding necessary judgments about means. An unrelieved diet of drilling on test-related exercises, for example, might produce higher scores but quench the spirit of learning.

There is a further complication. Teachers must worry not only about what kinds of learning occur, and how much, but also about *who* learns. Teaching inevitably must distribute opportunities to learn, but attention to aggregate outcomes often conceals distributional effects. Averages may rise, but not all students benefit equally. Those at the bottom of the distribution may be learning little. Pressures to produce results may impel teachers to concentrate on students most likely to learn, not on those most in need of special attention.

Ends cannot justify means in education because the interplay of means and ends is so complex. But as a practical matter, we must evaluate teaching on the basis of results because teaching is an instrumental activity aimed at producing learning. We would find it peculiar if a principal or teacher claimed to be doing wonderful things with children but was indifferent to their learning and could produce no evidence of it. This seems self-evident in a results-oriented culture such as ours, yet in two respects this perspective on teaching may be shortsighted.

First, state-of-the-art practice in a field may not guarantee results because knowledge connecting means to ends is imperfect and incomplete. Incompetence in the form of incorrect decisions and inadequate skill may produce poor results, but poor results may also be caused by lack of knowledge and an inability to control important contingencies affecting the outcome. In these latter cases, the practitioner cannot be held responsible. The brain surgeon may rightfully claim that the operation was a "success" (i.e., that the decision to operate was justified and that he or she skillfully employed the latest techniques) even though the patient died. Standards for best practice based on professional judgment are necessary even if they cannot guarantee results. With respect to such standards, a judgement about the practice becomes the appropriate measure, not reference to results alone.

Second, there are valued human activities in which we treat that outcome as incidental, concentrating instead on the quality of experience within the activity itself. Play is the classic example. Play fosters human growth and development, but that is not its raison d'être. Children and adults engage in play for the intrinsic pleasure of the experience. John Dewey reminds us that we must not sacrifice the playful aspects of learning to results-oriented methods. Must education have an aim? asked follow philosopher R.S.Peters, and he thought not.

Others philosophers have disagreed, but Dewey's thought is valuable in returning us to the immediacies of experience. We do care that schools and classrooms be humane and welcoming, and the school life be joyful, meaningful, and fulfilling. After all, children attend by law; they have no choice. Educators have a basic responsibility to provide for school *live* as well as for school *learning*. Here as elsewhere, Dewey sought to overcome dichotomy and dualism. Within pleasurable activity, the distinction between work and play dissolves; such solvent experience, he argued, is the ideal toward which education should tend.

But we also care about how school experiences live on in children and with what consequences for their future lives. If we rely on rational technical modes to pursue knowledge and skill, we can pursue other purposes only through mutual engagement with children in pleasurable and interesting activities. We cherish and seek to nourish such qualities as curiosity, creativity, and love of learning. But as the saying goes, these dispositions are "caught, not taught." Teachers convey and exemplify such qualities as much through their personhood as through their formal lessons. We should not be surprised, then, when research reveals that teachers think about their work in terms of activities, not results. All things considered, this is a wise and sensible orientation to teaching.

To judge teaching solely by its results is a mistake, yet results serve as teaching's anchor and compass. Teachers sail a sea of intense, vivid experiences with children. Their workdays and lives are emotionally demanding and fraught with uncertainty. A teacher's aims and objectives, purposes and intentions help direct his or her planning. A teacher's actual achievements, in the form of systematic and anecdotal evidence of student learning, help to modify and guide subsequent teaching.

Return now to the original puzzle, the relative absence of inspired and adventuresome teaching in our schools. Historians (e.g., Cuban, 1984, Cohen, 1987) have explored why this should be the case, indicating a range of factors. But I want to suggest that a contributing reason is a preoccupation with the results of instruction and a corresponding lack of attention to teaching itself. At first glance, this appears a peculiar indictment. After all, the point of teaching is to produce learning.

Recall, though, the arguments just made. As a practical matter we cannot ground judgments about teaching in results alone because we cannot fully specify nor accurately measure the outcomes of teaching, nor can we compare in a common scale of value the learning costs and benefits of particular strategies of instruction. As a professional matter, we can only employ best practices that reflect the current state of knowledge, however imperfect. And as a philosophical matter, we must value teaching for its intrinsic qualities. its contribution to communities of learning and to the lives of children.

The import of this argument is not that we should abandon testing and other devices to assess the outcomes of teaching. But standardized testing leads to standardized teaching, which cannot be healthy for children's growth and development. The implication is, rather, that we must fashion a public, appreciative framework for educational quality that conjoins attention to results with attention to teaching itself. We must begin to develop ways and means, process and language, to directly assess the quality of teaching and to persuade important publics that such methods are necessary and legitimate.

I propose that we supplement the prevailing emphasis on management by results with the creation of professional subcultures within schools based on *norms of conduct and standards of practice.* By norms of conduct I mean a range of moral and aesthetic judgments governing the role responsibilities of teachers. By standards of practice I mean the technical and procedural rules and guidelines that direct instruction. Such norms and standards can rise only out of dialogue and reflection based on the close observation of teaching. To create such norms and standards will require changes in what the public regards as evidence of good schools, in how administrators approach the management of teaching, and in the responsibilities teachers assume.

These are not minor adjustments. They will require time, inventiveness and the conviction that it is necessary to move in a new direction toward schools that value teaching in explicit and thorough-going ways. There questions that I can only begin to explore serve as starting points:

* What should be the form and substance of norms and standards for teaching?

* Through what practices should teachers and administrators begin to develop explicit norms and standards?

* What structural arrangements are necessary to support such practices?

Administrators have a crucial role both in interpreting teaching to the public and in creating processional subcultures that in turn generate norms and standards, Goals, results, and planning are the traditional tools of management, but these are insufficient. School administrators must also establish expectations and provide resources for frequent, regular observation of teaching by teacher, for ongoing deliberation about teaching, curriculum, evaluation, and learning, and for teacher writing about these matters. Teachers should regularly engage in the production of curricular materials and in critique of each others' handiwork. There should be video and audio tape equipment throughout schools, not only for student lessons, but to assist in the assessment of teaching itself.

Unlike many other professions, teaching leaves few traces: no precedents and decisions, no medical write-ups, no architectural or engineering feats. Consequently, there are few traditions of critical reflection on teaching, few codifications of the wisdom of practice. The starting point for an appreciation of teaching must be with the activity itself, but this means making teaching visible and accessible.

In every school, all teachers should spend some of their time trying out new practices, and some teachers should spend all of their time this way. This should be one hallmark of a teaching culture in schools, a commitment to practical inquiry and experimentation. We are not approaching that millennium in education when teachers may rely on settled practices and standard technologies in their work. They must become involved in efforts to invent new practices, to develop new materials, and to study children's development in collaboration with colleagues and with the support of administrators.

Teaching cultures need not be unique to individual schools, however. Promising programs and practices originate in many locals and should be available for scrutiny and trial. It must become a professional responsibility to stay abreast of developments in the field, to identify and try out approaches and materials developed elsewhere. Administrators should encourage and provide opportunity for teachers to identify and evaluate new materials instructional strategies, and programs.

Creative teaching is risky. Opening teaching to scrutiny is risky. And innovation is risky. Teachers must experiment with activities unfamiliar to themselves and to their students. They must open their classroom to observation and learn to become articulate about their practice. And they must reckon the costs of increased experimentation, collegiality, and openness. Departures from the norm may provoke uneasiness among, students, may cause disruptions, may threaten a teacher's control, may provoke disapproval from other teachers and administrators. Consequently, adventuresome teaching must be explicitly encouraged, rewarded, even expected, because powerful tendencies within schools press toward routine practices. Trust is critically important as is understanding within the community. Teachers cannot heedlessly experiment with children, they must approach new practices responsibly and inform and educate parents about their work.

There are a number of structural arrangements that might support norms of collegiality, experimentation, and deliberation, and practices of observation, constructive criticism, and development. A supervised induction for new teachers provides a valuable occasion for clarifying and transmitting norms and standards. Formal residencies can include requirements to demonstrate skill in employing a range of instructional techniques including, for example, simulations, small group work, collaborative goal structures, discovery learning and other innovative approaches. Regular classroom observation would be necessary as well, with mentor teachers taking on such responsibilities. Such residencies have value, not only for inducting newcomers, but for encouraging experienced teachers to become explicit about teaching practice.

A related structural support is the opportunity for teachers to assume advanced roles and responsibilities within schools. There must be ways to recognize teacher experience and expertise and to involve teachers in a variety of professional and leadership roles within schools. Such arrangements are already underway in many states and districts, going by names such as *career ladders, differentiated staffing,* and *mentor, master, or lead teachers.* These experiments are valuable but begin to suggest dangers in introducing bureaucratic ranks into the teaching profession. In the future, I believe light formalization will best serve, with teachers rotating through positions that are not permanent. Again, this approach requires skillful and flexible management to create such opportunities and to welcome the emergence of teacher leadership rather than regard it as a threat to management prerogatives.

A third promising arrangement is some form of association between schools and universities to create clinical settings for teacher education, to encourage collaborative inquiry, to establish status-enhancing adjunct positions for master teachers, and to join theory to practice in creating teaching norms and standards.

These suggestions regarding structure, practices, and the content of standards can only begin to suggest practical steps towards schools that value inspired teaching. Most of us believe that great teachers are "naturals"—gifted individuals born to be teachers. We think of a Marva Collins, a Sylvia Ashton-Warner. There are such people, to be sure, but we can systematically cultivate adventuresome teaching among many more teachers if we so choose. Phillip Schlechty is fond of saying that teachers know what is *expected* by what is *inspected* and what is *respected.* We have tended to inspect results alone and have failed to respect superb teaching. I can only hope that, in the future, one distinguishing characteristic of "successful" schools will be the presence of strong teaching—passionate, inspired, creative, idiosyncratic—nurtured within a strong professional subculture that takes pride in explicit norms and standards for teaching.

6

Flexibility and Authority in the Classroom

In its September 1987 issues, the *Phi Delta Kappan* published the eighteenth annual Gallup Poll of the public's attitudes toward public schools. Some of the results were offered a referendum on the success of the school reform movement that began with the appearance of *A Nation at Risk* in 1983. Did people think that schools had improved in the last five years? The answers were not encouraging. Only one in four questioned thought that education had gotten better.

But even if the public perception were accurate, would that be a fair evaluation of the reform movement? Many changes put in place have been called "reforms," but exactly what is it that they are supposed to achieve? Will we be getting something significantly better or just a spruced-up version of the old system?

What we have mainly seen so far has been a spate of state-level initiatives aimed at tightening up the looseness that crept into our schools in the freewheeling sixties and seventies. The message of this first round of reform was that students would no longer be allowed to graduate without taking solid academic courses. They would no longer be allowed to elect to "study" comic books or TV sitcoms instead of Dickens or Shakespeare. They would also have to measure up on basis competency tests, particularly in arithmetic and reading. Staying power would no longer be the main requirement for graduation; and in some places, even athletes—stars and scrubs alike—would be benched by bad report cards.

A parallel effort was made to shape up the teaching staff. Significant gains were made in salary levels aimed at improving recruitment and retention. In addition, states and communities that had once hired teachers solely on the basis of academic credits decided to try to find out if college diplomas meant anything and if teachers actually knew at least the basics of what they were supposedly trying to teach their students. In some states, veteran as well as beginning teachers were tested—in most cases on basic writing skills and on elementary level reading and arithmetic. Reform often meant demonstrating to taxpayers that they were getting at least some minimum value for their education tax dollar in their school staff.

Legislatures also tightened up the schoolhouse rule book. A wave of increased regulation, sometimes literally in massive tomes, cascaded from state capitals specifying what should be taught and when and from exactly what textbooks. Ironically school systems in the name of reform, thus adopted with a vengeance the highly centralized management style that industry was abandoning as reactionary and counter-productive.

Test teachers as well as students. Set tougher graduation and basic competency requirements. Mandate solid and clearly defined curriculums. But what is the likely impact of this "tightening up" process? Certainly it would be an improvement over what we had in 1983. In fact, success of this version of reform would mean going back to "the good old days", to the kind of schools that my generation knew in the forties and early fifties, which served many students quite well. But it also would mean going back to schools that had drop-out rates of up to 70 percent, to a time when a relatively small minority managed to earn a high school diploma, even though family structures were far more supportive than they are today.

Undoubtedly, many able youngsters who have been too casual about their education will respond positively to greater demands, but we can also easily imagine how other kids, who cannot function in the current system, will react to even tougher standards. Tightening the current system probably means a better education for some students, but increased frustration and failure for many other who, before reform, might have put in enough seat-time to get a diploma.

A look into the demographic crystal ball reveals other stumbling blocks down the road for efforts to save public education by rejuvenating the current system. Projections for the next five to seven years point to a major turnover in the teaching profession —replacing half of the nation's 2.2 million teachers, at least 200,000 new teachers each year. California alone, according to state education superintendent Bill Honig, will have to find at least 100,000 new teachers in the next five years. Putting it another way, just retain current staff levels, our schools will have to recruit and retain about 23 percent of each college graduating class for the next seven years! Is it reasonable or even desirable to expect that one institution in our society should be able to secure such a huge share of the nation's talent pool?

But the question is moot because nowhere near that number of undergraduates show an interest in teaching. Back in 1983, only 4 percent of all college students said that they were preparing to become teachers. This year, after all the reform measure sand publicity about improving our schools, this figure had risen to 6 percent, hardly within shouting range of the target number that our schools need. The picture looks even bleaker when we consider that the avowed aim of many reformers is to staff our schools with only the most highly qualified talent, which means that we would be faced with the hopeless task of recruiting close of half of the top half of every year's graduating class.

But how on earth did we manage to staff our schools in the good old days? Might the current reform movement learn something from the tactics of the past? The truth is that our schools were never very competitive and, over the years, benefited from social problems that often literally forced top-notch talent into the classroom. For example, traditionally, the largest pool of highly qualified personnel for our schools were women, who, fo r many generations, had few other career option. But a quick glance at the breakdown of college degrees awarded in recent years would show an immense shift of women into fields once closed to them—medicine, law, accounting, management, and computer technology. In the 1984-85 academic year, for example, 105,319 women received bachelor's degrees in business and management compared to 66,897 in education. This breakdown of economic and professional barriers has been a boon to women but a disaster for our schools.

Our schools gained another windfall from the great depression of the 1930s. Widespread unemployment made teaching attractive to many of the best and brightest. Competition for jobs any job—was intense; as the hard times dragged on, many of the most highly qualified candidates waited years for an appointment and, when it came, eagerly, accepted it. Schools were in the rare position of being able to pick and choose.

Years later, the selective service system provided another source of teaching talent. Many able young men were excused from military service by offering to teach in difficult-to-staff schools. They chose to struggle in the classrooms of our crumbling inner cities instead of fighting in the jungles of Vietnam.

But selective service has ended; there are many other career opportunities for educated people, and the economic and social barriers that once existed for women have been removed. Our schools will no longer get a "leg up" in recruitment from social problems. Perhaps for the first time in their history, they will have to face other employers in head-on competition for the available talent.

We need to ask ourselves how successful our reform initiatives will be in helping our schools meet this challenge. Consider the traditional strategies that employers use to recruit and retain staff. The first rule of the game, if you want top-level personnel, is to offer competitive salaries, equal to or more than the person you want to hire could get somewhere else. According to a recent national survey, " the average teacher *with a master's degree and 15 years' experience* (my emphasis) now makes $26,704," a year. This remember is the level achieved after five years of reform effort. In the decade before *A Nation at Risk,* teachers' salaries actually declined in terms of purchasing power.

Furthermore, are computer companies and accounting firms around the country promising new recruits fresh out of college (with a B.A., not an M.A.) that they'll be able to make over $26,000 in fifteen years? More likely, they're offering top candidates close to that or more as a starting salary.

Our schools need to add several thousand dollars to each teacher's salary to begin to bridge the gap between the education "industry" and the private sector. However, it takes only calculations to demonstrate that this is not likely to happen. Since we have 2.2 million teachers, every thousand dollar increase means a $2.2 billion increase in the nationwide education budget. If we took an average competitive professional salary to be about $35,000 and added pension and social security costs, we would face staggering $30 billion beyond what we now spend for education. The largest federal education program, Chapter 1, has an annual budget, of about $3 billion. Therefore, when we speak of increases to make teachers' salaries competitive with others professions, we're talking about a huge sum that is unlikely to be allocated to just one item in the overall education budget.

But even with substantial salary increases, schools will find it difficult to compete with the private sector, particularly in shortage areas like math and science. It's unlikely that corporate giants will allow themselves to come up short in the scramble for chemists, physicists, and computer experts. An illustration comes from the recent news report that business schools of prestigious universities were finding it difficult to fill all openings as faculty members hired in the 1950s retired, given the recruiting among both new college graduates and faculty by banks and other financial organizations.

Here's the bottom line: Though the reform movement has brought about significant and long-delayed improvements in teachers' salaries, it is unlikely that the new levels alone will offer sufficient incentives to enable us to restaff our schools as they are now structured with the caliber and quantity of candidates that we need for the twenty-first century.

But what if our schools significantly improve working conditions as well as raise salaries? Of course, a great deal can be done in this area, which, inevitably brings us back to money School plants in many places need to be repaired cleaned up, and made into civilized workplaces. Supplies need to be provided in sufficient quality and quantity. Teachers shouldn't continue to subsidize school systems out of their own pockets by supporting underfunded (or more likely, nonfunded) programs or by making up the shortfall of basic equipment and supplies.

The magnitude of the problem can be seen by looking at the item near the top of almost every teacher's personal agenda for change—class size. We've generally agreed that we don't want our youngsters to graduate from high school just knowing how to take multiple-choice tests, proficient only in filling in the right box or in checking the right square. We want them to be able to think to evaluate information, to be able to express themselves with fluency and clarity, to be able to defend a point of view with cogency and force. But these skills can only be acquired by frequent writing—not just by putting words on paper but by writing and rewriting with extensive and thoughtful feedback from teachers who have the time to read an reflect on their students' work, who do individual coaching to clarify thoughts and suggest alternate ways to express and support ideas.

But what's the real world like? The average high school teacher has five classes a day with 30 to 35 students in each—a total of at least 150 papers to read and grade for each writing assignment. If he or she spends just five minutes reading each paper and another five minutes making comments, the total time expended adds up to at least 25 hours of work—for one assignment! Added to the enormous amount of normal preparation time needed for daily lessons, an effective, continuing writing program is simply impossible.

Any reduction in class size would be welcome, but a 20 percent cut applied to the example above would still mean 20 hours of work instead of 25 for each writing assignment, a significant decline but still a crushing burden. And, remember, we're still talking about *minimum* time on task. How much would it take to do an optimum job? In short, a substantial reform of class size would still leave us with slightly better but essentially not very good working conditions, and most important, probably no significant change in education quality.

Again, arithmetic is fate. The numbers just don't add up for such an improvement. A 20 percent cut in class size would mean an equal increase in staff and education budget—a huge and utterly unrealistic increase for one item. And if, by some magic, the money were there, it is unlikely that we could begin to find that number of extra teachers because of the demographic facts of life I have already pointed out. The traditional reform approach won't even be able to recreate the "good" schools of the past.

Though a great deal of the tightening up so far has been a welcome corrective to the excesses of the recent past, it also has reinforced some of the worst characteristics of our education system. In the name of reform, we've had strengthened bureaucracies empowered to enforce rigid curriculums and mandated basic skills tests, which in the classroom, translates into more of what we've had before—lots of drill work and rote information processing from the teachers' lessons to the students' notebook and on to the periodic test.

Last spring the *Washington Post* (May 4,1987) reported the impact of "reform" in action, the implementation of a new systemwide basic skills test in the District of Columbia's schools. In a junior high school, students in the grades to be tested spent time "every school day since September" preparing for the exam," and, weeks before the test date, they "slogged through worn copies of the old test, answering multiple-choice questions on spelling, science, arithmetic and the always-knotty reading passages."

Call it reform, but it's suspiciously like the old system intensified, with a cramped and circumscribed vision of education. The system that many people are trying to spruce up in the name of reform locks our schools into well-worn paths of mediocrity and failure for far too many of our young people. It's a system that those with an eye exclusively on basic skills test scores can live with. Significantly, however, according to the Gallup poll that I referred to earlier, the greatest disapproval of the changes of the last five years came from inner-city, minority parents, whose children have been the most poorly educated. Perhaps the massage is that many parents see the crucial difference between cosmetic change and real reform.

There's no doubt that we can improve basic skills test scores with large doses of student prepping and sufficient fudging of statistics. But exactly what will we thereby accomplish ? Will young people have been engaged in their own education so that they're motivated and able to learn on their own? Will they have developed analytical powers to come to grips with important ideas? Will they have acquired the power of verbal and written communication so that they can express themselves with clarity and cogency? The truth is that these are not the usual by-products of an education in multiple-choice, test-taking strategies.

But there's another reform movement with another vision gaining momentum throughout the country. In an already much-quoted passage,the landmark Carnegie report, *A Nation Prepared* (1986), spoke of the need to educate "the vast majority" of our students "with achievement levels long thought possible for only the privileged few." It's an awesome challenge, but our national survival is at issue. And it's clearly a challenge that cannot be met by trying, like some of our reformers, to fine-tune the current system that regularly fails to reach anywhere from 40 to 60 percent of our young people.

Though there are models here and there that can teach us some valuable lessons about how to proceed, the reforms, that we need largely involve moving into uncharted territory. The time is ripe for bold departures. But whatever is done needs to be based on several fundamental principles.

1. Schools must be restructured to give teachers the greatest

possible flexibility in matching the student with the appropriate learning experience. We can't continue to expect the vast majority of pupils to do their best while spending most of their school time passively listening to an adult talk at them. Our drop-out and failure rates are proof of this. Students need to be directly and actively engaged in their own education—in small groups, in individual projects, in peer tutoring, and in one-on-one coaching sessions with teachers where written work can be effectively critiqued. We also need to break down the rigidity of our academic calendar. Some students who lack the discipline to tackle a whole semester's work might find success in mini-courses. Perhaps all five-year-olds are not ready for school in September. Some might do better if they started with another group in November of January and didn't have to compete with students who might be as much as eight to ten months older.

2. This increased flexibility needs to be complemented by a vastly expanded use of technology. Blackboard and chalk may be basic, but they can't be the end-all of our teaching tools as they are in too many of our classrooms. It's foolish for a teacher to lecture on the flora and fauna of the Galapagos Islands when the material can be more vividly and effectively presented by film or videotape. Computers may have been oversold in some areas, but we still haven't begun to tap the full potential of their real use in individualized learning.

3. We must solve the crisis in staffing our schools. In a recent report, Rand Corporation researchers warned that teacher attrition rates may soon reach their highest levels in 25 years. As I've argued, traditional strategies won't be able to cope with the magnitude of the problem. We need professional-level salaries as well as professional workplaces. As of now, the responsibilities of the 30-year veteran are exactly the same as those of the first-year beginner. There's almost no way to grow within the profession. We can't expect to recruit top-notch candidates to go into our classrooms unless we offer them the challenge and opportunity to exercise their creativity and judgment, the chance to control their working lives, the stimulation of frequent exchanges with their peers and a sense of being part of a vital intellectual community.

4. Such options will be possible, not only with a flexible school structure, but with an extensive and varied support staff. In a restructured school, teachers will need to be able to call on paraprofessionals, undergraduate "interns", and/or peer tutors. Our school will need to form alliances with private industry that can "lend-out " short-term" staff, particularly in such shortage areas as math and the sciences. We will have to explore a variety of staffing strategies if we want to break away from the rigidity of the prevailing system.

School improvement has been near the top of the national agenda for nearly five years with widespread support at all levels of society. But the latest Gallup poll should serve as a warning that the patience of the tax-payer has its limits. Most citizens are not impressed with what has been done in the name of reform. Attempting to fulfil our aspirations within the present structure can only lead to further disillusionment and perhaps, ultimately, to the abandonment of our current system of public education.

But a second wave of reform with far-reaching, revolutionary implications and vast potential has already begun. Communities like Rochester, New York; Hammond, Indiana; Toledo, Ohio, and Da County, Florida, have taken the first bold strides to restructure the teaching profession and remake our schools. Second-wave measures are not panaceas. We will see mistakes and false starts. But such measures are thoughtful challenges to the old rules and restraints. They are not commitments to bringing back the dubious good old days but commitments to creating something that we've never had before—schools that work for all our children.

7

Education and Values: Study, Practice, Example

Since ancient times, philosophers and scholars have known that values and education are indissolubly bound together. Their connection was so obvious and important that it was virtually impossible to imagine value-free education. Even if education did not transmit values explicitly and self-consciously, it did so implicitly and by example. Can anyone remember a distinguished teacher or philosopher, ancient or modern, who was morally neutral?

As a people we have come to understand that no nation that ignores values in education can hope to endure. No democracy that neglects values and education can expect to remain free. The reasons, though they should be obvious, bear repeating.

The American experiment in self-government is now two centuries old. Indeed, we are not only the oldest democracy in the world; we have an unbroken tradition of self-government marked by a long history of enlarging the franchise. When our experiment began, only white men of property could vote; today all citizens over 18 may do so. They may do so because we are convinced that all adults can responsibly exercise the franchise. They may do so if they are educated.

Philosophically, the reason for including values in education is clear enough: A democracy committed to the twin principles of equality and liberty must have an educated citizenry if it is to function effectively. By *educated* I mean not just people with a knowledge of basic skills, but people who are liberally educated. In this connection it is worth remembering the purpose of a liberal education: It is to suit men and women to lead lives of ordered liberty. It is the embodiment of the Jeffersonian vision of a free and equal people.

Such observations, of course, would hardly surprise the Founders. To them civic virtue was the *sine qua non* of a democratic republic, and it was in some large measure imparted by the formal institutions of society, among them schools. Indeed, without such norms, civilization itself is unimaginable. Born naked, ignorant, and full of appetites, each child must learn the facts and values of the culture anew. It is no surprise that formal schooling plays a major role in that process. Schooling and civic virtue cannot be separated.

In place of the hereditary aristocracy of the Old World, the New World, according to Thomas Jefferson, would witness the emergence of a natural aristocracy of talent. In a great democracy, as all men are equal before God and the law, so too are all men free to develop their talents to the fullest. This elegant and radical idea survives to this day, and for its full development, the people of a democracy must be educated. As Lord Brougham said, "Education makes a people easy to lead, but difficult to drive; easy to govern, but impossible to enslave."

The ancient Greeks, from whom we inherit our intellectual and educational traditions, knew that there was one purpose for education and one only: to fit man to live in the *polis*. And the key to life in the *polis* is values, "civic virtue"; without it the *polis*, the state itself, would flounder. They had the insight to know how one acquires civic virtue. Their threefold lesson is as true today as it was then. It is study, example, and practice.

First, values are acquired by study, knowledge acquired didactically. Teachers teach and students learn. Study requires submission to the discipline of learning. Second, values are acquired by example. Virtuous men and women by example communicate values to the young and to their fellows. Third, and perhaps most important, values are acquired by practice. Virtue is acquired by behaving virtuously.

Long before the excellence movement there were two broad schools of thought in such matters. One is the vision of school as agent of the state, familiar enough to any one who cares to peer beyond the iron curtain. John Stuart Mill, who was spared the excesses of modern totalitarian and authoritarian regimes, thought that no other objective could characterize government schooling. Government education, whether the dominant power be a priesthood, monarchy, or majority of the existing generation, is "a mere contrivance for moulding people to be exactly like one another and as the mould in which it casts them is that which pleases the predominant power in the government...it establishes a despotism over the mind...."

By way of contrast there is the perspective of a supporter of government as the instrument of civic virtue, Simon Bolivar. Addressing the Congress of Angostura, he solemnly observed: "Let us give to our republic a fourth power with authority over the youth, the hearts of men....Let us establish this Areopagus to watch over the education of the children...to purify whatever may be corrupt in the republic...."

There is, however, a less extreme way to think about education and civic virtue in a democracy. How should a free people inculcate those values and attitudes essential to public welfare, domestic tranquility, and the pursuit of happiness? How can order and freedom be reconciled? The task, while not easy, is not impossible. And the American experience of the past century and one-half with public education—or the education of the public—is instructive.

What are the values of civic virtue? First, explicit knowledge, mastered to the point of habit, about the rights and responsibilities of citizenship, and the opportunities and obligations imposed by a constitutional republic. It is knowing, as sociologist Morris Janowitz observed, that the corollary of the right to trial by jury is the obligation to serve on a jury when called. It is knowing that one man's freedom ends where another's begins. It is knowing that rights are earned and must be protected if they are to survive. It is knowing that Supreme Court Justice Oliver Wendell Holmes was right when he observed that "taxes are what we pay for civilized society."

What is it our public schools should do to teach values? What must children acquire to make them virtuous citizens? Let me look first at example, then study, then practice.

The most striking example of citizenship in all of history was offered by Socrates. He accepted the hemlock cup not because he believed himself guilty of corrupting the youth of Athens, but to demonstrate the supremacy of law. His wisdom and his courage are captured by John Ruskin in words that contain the essence of my point: "Education does not mean teaching people what they do not know...It is a painful, continual, and difficult work to be done by kindness, by watching, by warning, by precept, and by praise, but above all by example."

As a practical matter, this means that our schools must be staffed by moral men and women who care about their calling and their craft. By the pure force of personality they must communicate their sense of commitment to their students. There is no mystery as to who these people are. They are the teachers we each remember, the teachers who made a difference in our own lives. The problem is not identifying them after the fact, but before the fact. They are the teachers who are connected to their disciplinary traditions, who are broadly and deeply educated, and who believe in the life of the mind.

These are not empty homilies. There is an internal dynamic to study and scholarship, and there are canons of the profession that themselves embody the values of a democratic society. They include honesty, fidelity, accuracy, fairness, tolerance for diversity, flexibility, and a willingness to change when new evidence is presented. Indeed, what we expect of our better teachers is precisely the set of traits that we associate with civic virtue.

Another name I use to describe this cluster of attributes and the outcomes they help foster is *the invisible curriculum.* It is the message sent by teachers to students about what is right and what is wrong, what is acceptable and what is not. A school, for example, that sets low standards sends a powerful message: Nothing much matters, get by. That is a dangerous message to give a young person because it programs him for failure. The invisible curriculum undergirds and reinforces the students' visible curriculum.

It has become fashionable in certain circles to think that education is a *process,* a set of skills divorced from their substantive context. That is not true. Education is contextual. It is a substantive experience which requires, among other things, learning about the great documents of citizenship. At a minimum these include an acquaintance with Aristotle's *Politics and Ethics,* Plato's *Republic,* the Magna Carta, *The Prince* by Machiavelli, *An Essay Concerning Human Understanding* by John Locke, the Declaration of Independence, the Tenth *Federalist Paper,* the United States Constitution, John Stuart Mill's *On Liberty,* the Gettysburg Address, Lincoln's Second Inaugural Address, and Martin Luther King's "Letter from Birmingham Jail." Education is an empty concept if it is stripped of the values these documents embody. As King reminds us, "Freedom is never voluntarily given by the oppressor; it must be demanded by the oppressed." This is first and foremost a normative statement, a statement of values.

To be fully educated, the student must master a body of knowledge, fact, myth, history, anecdote, not as an exercise in memory, but as an exercise in understanding and critical thought. History and context are important to education both for themselves and as the instrumentality by which people learn to think and to reason. It is simple but true: People learn to think by thinking and thinking hard. That is the essence of the Socratic dialogue, the most enduring and important teaching technique ever devised.

Think of the centerpiece of the Fifth Amendment as simply a phrase to be recapitulated without an understanding of its underlying meaning: "nor shall be compelled in any criminal case to be a witness against himself." Without an understanding of its purpose and its historical context, it is truly nonsense. Why should a suspected criminal not have to testify against himself? protecting all of us from testifying against ourselves emerged from a long and bitter history of the rack and thumb screw—if a man may be compelled to testify against himself, who is to say no to the torturer? Certainly not the victim. Freedom from self-incrimination is no more and no less than freedom from the Inquisitor and the tools of his trade. It is a strange thing in a century so convulsed by violence of every kind that this simple truth is frequently overlooked when people "take the Fifth." It may be the single most important protection a free people enjoy.

In exploring the idea of values and education we must remember that values are a part of our world that is not scientifically derived. They include such human but unscientific attributes as love, loyalty, courage, devotion, piety, and compassion. These attributes give dimension, scope, and meaning to being human. It is precisely with these attributes that great literature concerns itself.

Let me draw upon a particularly telling and appropriate example, Mark Twain's *Huckleberry Finn,* published more than a century ago. It is arguably the greatest American novel, a book of such importance that no American who has not read it can be considered educated. What makes this book important? Its scope and sweep, certainly, but above all, its values. In shape it is a book for the masses. Like the Bible or the *Iliad* it tells a universal story, accessible to all. Just as it contains much with which to agree, it contains much that shocks, provokes, and even offends. As a consequence, reading the book and discussing it in a classroom require sensitivity and discretion. It is not a book to be taken lightly.

It is interesting that the book is attacked today just as it was when first released. The far right believes Huck is venal at best, and hostile to religion at worst. They say his language is abominable, his behavior unacceptable. In sum, he is a poor example. The left is even more outspoken in its hostility to Huck. They level against him the worst of modern epithets: racist.

I will stipulate to this: Twain's purpose was to subvert the state, undermine the morals of the young, and challenge the smugness and complacency of the American *haute bourgeoisie.* To this accusation I plead Twain guilty. And this is precisely the power of the book: to confront the conventional wisdom. Twain railed against the organized religion of the day and its sanctimonious piety and hypocrisy. Indeed, he found organized society, particularly the state, the cause rather than the cure for social ills. Huck and Jim, children of nature, could escape the corrupting forces of contemporary life only by physical escape.

So far as we can tell, Twain really believed that society was a sentence and the only hope was escape. The development of this idea in *Huckleberry Finn* is the best known of Twain's repeated efforts to deal with it. If this interpretation of Twain is correct, as I believe it to be, he is far more dangerous than either the left or right wings know. He is an enemy of the state.

Whether or not he should be read by callow youths, then, becomes a question with meaning. The direction assumed by other great works across the ages is the same. While the first purpose is to entertain, the more important purpose is to instruct. Such literature is almost never the servant of the state nor the advocate of the status quo.

Jean DuBuffet, champion of *l'art brut,* the raw or unschooled art, in a splendid twist on Plato asserted that art was subversive, that the state should attempt to suppress it, and that the artist worked best and most effectively when he was disdained by the prevailing culture. That is, in fact, a rather exaggerated version of my hypothesis here. Suffice it to say that the artist should question, at a minimum, the conventional wisdom and make the *bourgeoisie* uncomfortable.

Without dwelling on Twain, it is useful to consider great literature in general to see if the example is idiosyncratic. Are there common threads? The direction assumed by great literature across the ages is the same. While its first purpose is to entertain, its more important purpose is to instruct. It provides examples of courage, strength, and love. It shows the effects of hubris, greed, and the will to power. It reveals transcendent accomplishment and abject failure. Such literature is almost never the servant of the state or the advocate of the status quo. Great literature challenges assumptions, it breaks with the conventional wisdom.

Not all great books are offensive, or irreverent, or hostile to the state, but they challenge the conventional wisdom, they provoke the reader, they insist upon engagement with the subject. This is even true of science, particularly in its early stages when it is concerned with breakthroughs in basic knowledge. Galileo, Kepler, and Darwin are only the best known examples.

The controversial nature of a work, then, is a product of its power and authenticity, and it is for this reason that the inexperienced reader will frequently find the great book difficult—it is often very tough sledding. It is tough sledding because it raises fundamental questions about right and wrong. For the inquiring mind, it induces an interior Socratic dialogue.

At issue in the teaching of values is an error of judgment that continues to plague our schools. An assumption was made, in all good faith, that our schools could be value-free, neutral, and objective; this would defuse the potentially explosive question of which values to teach and how to teach them. This vision of American education is an old one.

In the nineteenth century what was described as value-free education was really nonsectarian Protestantism. It was not quite cumenism, but a robust Unitarianism. Indeed, it is no accident that the early public school reformers were visionary and romantic Unitarians, builders who would use the public schools to uplift and transform each generation. As Horace Mann, with a striking sense of modernity, said in his *Annual Report to the Board of Education* in 1848; "If all the children in the community from the age of four to that of seventeen could be brought within the reformatory and elevating influence of good schools, the dark host of private vices and public crimes....might....be banished from the world."

When it came to values education, Mann, as well as his

supporters and colleagues, had little problem identifying what schools should doe. They knew that most teachers were poorly trained, and they were the inheritors of a classical tradition that brooked little interference. In essence, the curriculum chose itself. So it was in the late nineteenth century that the McGuffey *Reader* enjoyed unparalleled success. It was full of pious homilies and entreaties to civic and religious virtues, the values widely shared by the community that patronized the public schools. In the nineteenth century, the patrons were almost exclusively white Protestants. The emergence of a highly diverse, democratic, and pluralistic modern society means that we can to longer rely on either the classical curriculum or the Protestant consensus of the nineteenth century.

In an attenuated way this disciplinary tradition does exist in the best public and private college preparatory schools. In these institutions, for example, teachers are free to choose Dryden or Donne, Spencer or Marlowe, Shakespeare or Cervantes, Twain or Hawthorne—but the freedom to choose is nearly ephemeral, because the educated person, the student, must eventually read all of them.

What has happened in American education, of course, is the virtual abandonment of the disciplinary tradition. Instead of vertical integration, elementary and secondary schools are organized horizontally. They are not only characterized by self-contained classrooms, they are self-contained organizations with few links to the outside world. Great bands of children are grouped by age, and they are given "problem areas" to study. Communications skills replace English, social studies replaces history and geography; is it any surprise that bachelor living and power volleyball enter the curriculum? Is it any wonder that there are periodic attempts to purge Huck Finn from the classroom? With no intellectual and disciplinary anchor, the school is subject to the fads and vicissitudes of the moment. When the watchwords of the school become "value neutrality" "relevance," and "relativity" anything goes.

Nothing is imposed on anyone, except the notion that there are two sides to every question. The philosophy of the ancient Greeks and the great revealed religions, both based on moral absolutes, no longer provide answers. Not even the existential answer that teachers know more than students can be offered with conviction. It is for these reasons that the disciplinary tradition is essential.

Let me turn briefly to my final point: *practice.* "Happiness," Aristotle tells us, "is activity of the soul in accord with perfect virtue." We achieve this state by practice. Ironically, it is not so much in the exercise of our rights that we learn this, but in meeting our corresponding obligations. It is through submission to a higher principle that we learn to appreciate the importance of our hard-won rights.

At the level of friend and family, *practice* means satisfying the reciprocal demands that loyalty and filial responsibility place upon us. At the level of the community, it means meeting minimum standards of civility and good conduct. More than just obeying the law, it means accommodation to unspoken standards of behavior. At the level of the state, it means honoring the full and explicit demands of citizenship, from honesty in paying taxes, to citizen participation, to the ultimate sacrifice for a higher good in time of mortal danger.

At the level of the school, *practice* means doing what is expected and doing it well. But it could and should mean much more. It could and should mean *service,* both to the school and to the community. Although an old idea in private education, service is just now being taken seriously in the public sector.

The North Carolina School of Science and Mathematics, one of the nation's only public boarding schools, enrolls some of the best and brightest youngsters in North Carolina. There is a special graduation requirement that says no student may graduate without performing three hours a week of school service and four hours a week of community service. Students fron NCSSM spend time in nursing homes, orphanages, day care centers, and hospitals. And they do so week in and week out.

Every high school student in the United States should be expected to perform community service as a condition of graduation. No one is so poor or so elevated as to not profit from it, for that is surely its purpose. The help these young people provide, while important, is the least of what they do. What is really important is that they are learning through practice the habits of service. That is the very foundation of civic virtue and the personal satisfaction it can provide.

What this means, of course, is that we cannot avoid the question of curriculum. What we teach we value, and what we value we teach. The curriculum, both visible and invisible, is value-laden. What is it we need to know as Americans, to have both a shared sense of community and a shared destiny?

At the same time, we need the support, solace, and integrity of the smaller, organic communities of which we are naturally a part. No one can be a member of a "family" of 240 million people. We can be citizens, and owe obligations and expect rights to flow from this larger body politic, but the kinds of association that most of us find deeply satisfying flow from smaller units of organizations.

Any curriculum—particularly a "core" curriculum—must reconcile the demands of a continental democracy and the need to belong to a more intimate community. It must reflect the values of the whole and the part, respecting both while supporting the individual.

The need is acute because in the final analysis "excellence" in any endeavor is a solitary pursuit, requiring self-discipline and commitment. Excellence also assumes many forms music, art, the quantitative disciplines, languages, and the humanities. And over the life of a student the pursuit of excellence calls for progressively greater specialization and more complete immersion in the peculiarities of a given discipline.

This is not to say that a core curriculum cannot coexist with specialization: It can. It is just more difficult to pull it off successfully. And this raises the most important question of all. If curriculum is central and values are central to the curriculum, who will choose, and of what will the curriculum consist? If it is chosen by the wise and judicious, the penetrating and the discerning, the discriminating and the disciplined in short, by you and me—the curriculum will be a wonder to behold.

But if it is chosen by the ideologues of the left or right, the Babbitts and buffoons of American intellectual life, it will be a disaster. The fear of the latter is a real one, as anyone who has read Frances FitzGerald's study of U.S. history texts must admit. Anti-intellectualism in the United States is an old, powerful, and even honored tradition, and it is not at all clear that the excellence movement will, even over the long haul, change that.

Lurking beneath the surface of any discussion about the quality of American education is the nagging suspicion that we already have the schools that we both want and deserve. We do have citizen control; we do have a voice in what our schools do and how they do it, however attenuated it may be. Perhaps, after all is said and done, Americans prefer football to the life of the mind. That, after all, is what values are all about.

The life of the school, then, is defined by what is taught, and the life of the student is defined by what is learned.

What has this to do with education and values? A good deal, I think, because we are what we value, and schools cannot escape this simple truth. And at the heart of the excellence movement—if indeed it has a heart lies the conviction that it makes a difference what children are taught and what they learn.

In conclusion, let me offer the quintessential and timeless expression of values and education that is carved in stone on the B'nai B'rith headquarters in Washington, D.C. The words never cease to move me. "The world stands on three foundations; study, work, and benevolence."

8

Equity Versus Excellence

Why Do Some Reforms Persist?

Certain Educational Reforms have been adopted over and over again to solve particular problems in schools. We can draw three conclusions from this phenomenon. First, since a solution should end a problem, and these reforms have been used again and again, they have failed to remove the problems they were intended to solve. Second, the problems defined as important were either not the problems that needed to be solved and the solutions (reforms) were inappropriate, or the solutions were designed to correct different problems that the ones identified. In short, the problems and solutions are mismatched. Third, perhaps the problems were instead persistent dilemmas involving hard choices between conflicting values. Such choices seldom get resolved but rather get managed; that is, compromises are struck until the dilemmas reappear. I will explore these three statements.

The current passion among states for a traditional education, one in which every student studies a core of academic subjects, is one example of a recurring solution dating back over a century. It is a solution to the problem of how to balance societal values of excellence and equity in tax-supported public schools enrolling children of different abilities social classes, religions, and racial and ethnic groups.

Requiring academic core subjects does not solve a problem but rather is a compromise to a fundamental dilemma in American schools over conflicting values of excellence and equity in providing an equal education to all children. Solutions are supposed to end problems; however, conflicts over values (dilemmas) produce compromises that are struck and restruck over time.

The situations defined as problems in the arena of public policy are really value conflicts that surface frequently as school issues get dealt with as a series of reform in structures, rules, staffing, and programs (i.e., solutions) and then disappear from view—for a while. The conflict in values reappears when larger social, political, and economic issues call attention to the school's role in wrestling with these prized but competing values. Hence, there is constancy in reform and repeated efforts to restrike a political consensus over these societal values. When a consensus is reached at the rhetorical level, however, it often breaks down at the level of making policy decisions about programs and allocating resources.

The conflicting values of excellence and equity, proxies for this culture's fundamental values of individual success and group interests, have been dealt with separately, redefined, and combined over the last century and a half to cope with the highly charged emotions and national goals connected to these values. No consensus on which of these values is more or less important or how they can be incorporated easily into public policies involving schools has produced lasting compromises in curricular policy-making. Curricular changes come and go.

Finally, these periodic curricular reforms, inevitably responding to larger socioeconomic and political issues over the last century, have been accommodations to this conflict of highly prized values. A brief description of these compromises would help.

In the mid-nineteenth century, when the idea of tax-supported public schools had become widespread, the prevailing opinion was that all students should be exposed to the same curriculum—the common school. The concept of equality mandated that the conditions of schooling be the same for all. Equity and access to schooling was the ideal, although certain groups of students were excluded in these years. In the post-Civil War decades, however, urban schools, especially high schools, responded to ballooning numbers of students drawn from many social classes and ethnic groups by expanding the numbers of available courses. High schools made erratic and unsystematic efforts to differentiate the content and instruction of classes to match the differences in students. The patchwork quilt of course offerings in grammar and high schools made it correspondingly difficult for colleges and universities to make admissions decisions.

In 1893, the report of the Committee of Ten on Secondary School Studies (sponsored by the National Education Association) recommended for all high schools an academic core of four years of English, three years of history, science, mathematics, and a foreign language. Chaired by Harvard President Charles Eliot the committee urged that: "Every subject which is taught at all in a secondary school should be taught in the same way and to the same extent to every pupil as long as he pursues it, no matter what the probable destination of the pupil may be, or at what point his education is to cease" (in Krug, 1961, p. 87)

By the time of the First World War, the Committee of Ten's goal to reduce the variety of courses and standardize both the time allotted to a subject and the teaching method had been fulfilled; its recommendations were mainstream practice. What was nce god for those going to college was now defined as good for all. During the same period, however, another generation of reformers—opposed to Eliot and like-minded reformers—sought to resurrect from earlier decades the multiple courses of study tailored to different needs of students, since such variety was more in keeping with their definition of democracy and equal education (Cremin, 1961, Krug, 1964)

In 1918, another national report (also sponsored by the National Education Association) *The Cardinal Principles of Secondary Education* set forth another generation's manifesto challenging the concept of a single best curriculum for all students. progressives saw varied curricula designed for different futures as a way for secondary schools to concentrate attention on fulfilling each student's potential while preparing that student for his or her probable niche in society. Elementary schools continued to provide the same curriculum to all students.

Over the next three decades, the gospel of secondary school progressives produced the comprehensive high school with varied curricula for students headed toward diverse futures. Vocational education, college preparatory courses, business classes and other curricula expanded the familiar academics of earlier years (Kurg,1964; Powell, Farrar,& Cohen, 1985)

By the early 1950s' the earlier solution of varied curricula that had replaced the single academic course of study became the target for even another generation of reformers who saw anti-intellectual flabbiness and a diminished concern for excellence in nonacademic high school courses. Arthur Bestor's *Educational Wastelands: The Retreat from Learning in Our Public Schools* (1953) and Albert Lynd's *Quackery in the Public Schools* (1953), for example, blasted the low academic standards and the quality of teaching in high schools. Seldom were blasts directed at elementary schools, however, where the common core curriculum persisted.

With evidence of the Soviet Union's technological gains orbiting the earth in 1957, further barrages of criticism accelerated concern for the mindlessness of so many high school courses. Generated by fears for national security federal legislation (the National Education Defense Act, 1958), James Bryce Conant's report on high schools (1959) and new academic programs spilled over schools. More and more high school raised academic standards by increasing the number of courses in math, science, and foreign languages. Advanced placement courses were established. Subsidized by foundations and federal funds, academics constructed new curricula based upon the nature of the disciplines and how scientists practiced biology, physics, math and the social sciences. Few of these attacks, however, questioned seriously the previous solution—the comprehensive high school itself—as being inappropriate (Conant, 1959).

But by the mid-1960s and later, political and social movement aimed at freeing the individual from bureaucratic constraints and helping the poor, especially ethnic and racial minorities, swept across schools. If desegregation, compensatory education, and magnet schools became familiar phrases, so did free schools, open classrooms, and flexible scheduling. Many (but not all) of the previous decade's academic reforms evaporated by the early 1970's, as efforts redoubled to differentiate courses and schools to accommodate low-income and minority children with little access to academic curricula. Special programs, alternative schools, and new curricula dotted the urban and suburban school landscape in efforts to recapture students who had been either relegated to the margins of a high school education or pushed out. Concern for access and equal treatment led to further differentiation in curricula (Powell et 1985,pp.281-300; Revitch, 1983, pp. 228-226).

By the late 1970s and early 1980s, a renewed call for a core academic curricula in high schools available to all students had again surfaced. *A Nation at Risk* (1983), written by the National Commission on Excellence in Education, urged readers to demand higher academic standards and a common curriculum of their schools. State after state raised its graduation requirements and more and more students took chemistry geometry and foreign languages; fewer students registered for vocational courses. Mortimer Ader's *Paideia Proposal* (1982) renewed discussion of the Great Books curriculum, and calls for a return to traditional curricula have marked the early to mid-1980's debate on the refrom of schooling. In California, a pacesetter among the states in raising graduation requirements of core academic subjects voters responded warmly to State Superintendent Bill Honig's message for traditional schooling. A graduate of an academically selective. San Francisco high school Honig (1985) said: "A traditional education worked for us; why shouldn't we give at least as good a shot at the common culture to today's children" (p. 55)

For almost a century this enduring debate over whether all students should take one academic curriculum or varied ones has shuttled back and forth between proponents of different versions of what an "equal education" means in a democracy. The values of equity and excellence, each defined in numerous ways, are entangled in any definition of an equal education. The invention of the comprehensive high school in the first quarter of this century fashioned a workable compromise that both the lay public and professional educators endorsed. But the compromise could not prevent national fears about foreign and domestic policies from penetrating the schools. Each time this debate occurred, administrators and specialists created new courses of study and curriculum guides. New texts appeared. These changes, however were again refashioned compromises between competing values of excellence and equity, between the interests of the individual and those of the larger group.

The shifting high school curriculum since the mid-nineteenth century (with many fewer shifts at elementary level) reveals the competing values embedded in the common school curriculum, compared to the differentiated courses of study a generation later, subsequently modified by a partial return to the core academic subjects under the Committee of Ten in the mid-1890s. And so it went through the twentieth century as well. The comprehensive high school, a political and educational compromise, has adapted to the external pressures seeking to restrike the original compromise over a half century ago. These repeated efforts to come to grips with the external demands for the school to serve conflicting values only mirror inherent tensions in the larger culture.

In the 1980s, the debate has been renewed. Calls for excellence have been translated into higher graduation requirements more homework a longer school year, and the drive to raise test scores—to make everyone above average. And changes have again occurred. The comprehensive high school again tilts toward the excellence side of the debate, but the institution itself persists as a compromise. Yet the current concern in the big cities for huge percentages of students who leave school early is both a familiar theme over the last century and an early signal for another major effort to adjust the comprehensive high school to the competing values.

Of what policy use is this answer to the initial question that I posed: Why do so many reforms, repeatedly appear as solutions to school problems? I have argued that what appear as solutions (e.g., tougher graduation requirements) are really tactical moves to ease political tensions over the role of schools in meeting two competing values. The basic political compromise was worked out in the early decades of this century, that is, the elementary schools as the traditional home for a common curriculum and the comprehensive high school as a place offering varied courses of study to deal with the high percentages of students staying on to graduation—rising from one in five to three of every four students nationally. This compromise has successfully managed the hard choices embedded in the dilemma of conflicting values. No solutions here, but important accommodations. Thus knowing the difference between a problem that can be solved and a dilemma presenting difficult choices can help both policymakers and practitioners avoid the excesses of a can-do pragmatism that so frequently leads to ill-defined educational problems and mismatched solutions posing as school reforms.

Of equal importance to policymakers is the clear understanding that the comprehensive high school itself is a durable compromise to this dilemma that has worked. By "worked" I mean that the institution has produced the highest percentages of public school graduates in the world and has managed to accommodate each successive wave of reform energies directed at both equity and excellence. The solution of the comprehensive high school has persisted, I believe, because it contains the ideology, structures, and minimum resources to embrace competing values.

Whether it will continue depends upon a clear understanding of the differences between problems and dilemmas, between solutions and compromises. The present generation of state and federal policymakers active in the reform movement has accepted the historic compromise and wishes to make existing schools lean more to their preferences for what they call excellence. Few if any, have questioned the very compromise itself. Perhaps the time has come to seriously examine the available alternatives that can compete with the comprehensive high school as a workable way of accommodating tensions between competing values.

9

The Future of Small, Rural Schools

Regardless of whether the impetus for educational reform stems from the pen of a scribbling academic, an opportunistic politician, or a faceless bureaucrat, a reform movement proceeds in steps, involves many actors playing a wide variety of roles, and can evolve to such a degree that it is difficult to discern the original intent from the ultimate impact. The point is not to stress the self-evident fact that reforms can be transmuted in various ways as they proceed from perceptions of need to concrete programs for improvement. Rather, the point is to note that these modifications can also be made to serve the interests of the persons doing the modifying. More broadly still, the point is that the impetus for reform can be captured and put to uses not intended by those who came earlier in the reform process. Indeed, drives to reform can be turned to purposes patently contrary to the ideas that gave rise to them. It is well, then, to keep an eye on reformers, lest a reform popular, and sensible at its early states be transmuted into practices far removed from original intentions.

A good case in point is the impact that the current reform movement, an effort now codified into law in many states, is having on small, rural schools. There is reason to believe that this reform movement is being used by state education officials to engineer another round of school district consolidations in rural regions. Such a development would be painfully ironic, since in runs counter to virtually all recent research on school size and to the expressed objectives of some of the reformers themselves.

The Reform Movement And School Size

While the modern reform movement has numerous themes and is difficult to capture in a single statement, many of its central concerns focus on the nature and level of schooling outcomes. Making schools offer a better mix of courses (e.g., requiring more science and mathematics) at higher levels of achievement (e.g., testing for minimum competency) at less cost to taxpayers (e.g., paying teachers according to their actual contributions) are all consistent with the thrust of the reform movement. This is the "hard " side of school reform *A Nation at Risk* (National Commission on Excellence in Education, 1983) is paradigmatic.

In addition to the "stiffen academic requirements and make schools more accountable" theme, there is a second, "softer" dimension to the reform movement. Here the focus is on the social and moral side of student's schooling (e.g., reducing dropout rates) on greater cooperation among teachers and administrators (e.g., developing a climate of trust and shared responsibilities), and on a stronger role for parents and building administrators in school affairs (e.g., decentralizing decision-making.) Lightfoot's *The Good High School* (1983) is illustrative.

The hard and soft themes in the reform movement have different implications for the future of small rural schools. As we shall show in the following section, in some quarters, there is a widespread and deeply entrenched belief that large size is a prerequisite for a cost-effective, diverse, and specialized curriculum. Moreever, there is a parallel belief that greater standardization and accountability follow from dividing a state into a small number of similarly organized, relatively large units. According to this belief, the fewer districts the better for the sake of exercising state oversight. Thus, expanding educational offerings and making educators more accountable to the state—the hard dimension of the reform movement —is very much consistent with a "larger is better" point of view.

In sharp contrast, researchers have concluded that large schools have adverse effects on certain aspects of the education and social development of youth. Beginning with the seminal work of Barker and Gump (1964), it has become clear that students in smaller schools participate more actively in the extracurriculum, have better, self-concepts, and exhibit lower levels of alienation. (See Hamilton, 1983, for a thorough review of this research.) More over, there is some evidence that small schools are more closely tied to their communities (Carlsen $ Dunn, 1981; Peshkin,1978) and operate with less hierarchical, more collegial decision-making structures than do their larger counterparts (Dunn, 1977).

Thus, the two central themes of the modern school reform movement have contradictory implications for the future viability of small rural schools. In light of this, it is not surprising that modern reformers have had little to say explicitly about size or small rural schools per se. In the few instances where size is mentioned (Boyer, 1983, Goodlad, 1984, Lightfoot, 1983; Powell. Farrar, Cohen, 1985), big schools are either viewed as a clear-cut source of undesirable outcomes (as in Goodlad, 1984) or as the source of a dilemma wherein officials must balance the opportunities for an expanded curriculum against the drawbacks for student social development or increased parental involvement (as in Boyer, 1983).

Further, the leaders of the reform movement have not explicitly rejected the long-standing belief that a more diversified curriculum can be more cost-effectively offered in larger school systems. Instead, they seem more concerned about the nature of the specialization that is offered. For example, Powell and his colleagues decry the lack of coherence in high school courses; they do not question the virtue of offering a diversified curriculum (Powell, Farrar, Cohen , 1985). Moreover several reformers suggest ways of achieving the advantages of small size within the context of large districts and schools. Even Goodlad (1984), who is most explicit is his denunciation of large schools, notes that creating five or six small schools within a single large one means that each can benefit from sharing common facilities, such as libraries and gymnasiums. He concludes; "It is not impossible to have a good large school; it simply is more difficult" (p.309). Boyer (1983) makes similar points. Such suggestions imply that whatever the virtues of small schools, they need not be lost in the process of creating large ones.

We conclude that the modern reform movement sends two inconsistent messages regarding school size. By not repudiating the idea that large size facilitates an enriched academic curriculum and by explicitly endorsing an expansion of academic opportunities through increasing graduation requirements, the hard side of the movement tacitly supports the further consolidation of small rural school districts. However, by simultaneously stressing the importance of the social outcomes of schooling; the necessity of a cooperative, caring climate; and the need for vastly increased parent involvement, its soft side helps to undercut the case for consolidation.

Which of these themes will prevail in rural areas depends on more than their relative strength. Current reforms must be viewed in light of the legacy of past reforms, particularly those that have been directed uniquely at small rural schools. We consider this history next.

The Legacy Of Rural School Reform

The history of rural education in this country provides remarkably compelling evidence against the view that educational institutions are highly resistant to change. The successive waves of school consolidations that washed over rural regions in the last half-century have been among the most successful educational reforms ever undertaken—if one defines *success* as the realization of the reformers' goal. They have transformed rural education, replacing tiny schools serving a few students and a singly village with large, complex organizations serving hundreds or even thousands of pupils from several distinct communities.

The magnitude of this transformation is easy to document. For example, the number of school districts in the United States, declined from 128,000 in 1930 to slightly over 14,000 today. In the same period, the number of one-room elementary schools went from nearly 150,000 to fewer than 1,500 (Sher Tompkins, 1977). But to appreciate the real magnitude of the transformation, one must, remember that this wholesale abolition of local school boards meant in fact, the abolition of thousands of local governments. Further, these government were not obscure entities performing some trivial social task; they were governmental bodies that daily touched the lives of citizens in a critically sensitive area, the welfare of their children.

The rationale offered for this massive reform rested on the idea that larger schools and school districts were more equitable and more efficient. They were more equitable because small schools denied rural students equaliity of educational opportunity by not providing the variety of programs offered by larger institutions. Similary, larger schools were more efficient because they could offer any given program at a lower per-pupil expense, or they could offer a wider variety of programs at no greater expense.

Both the equity and efficiency argument are highly problematic. For almost two decades, accumulating research suggests that making large rural schools from small rural schools does not dependably result in either greater equity or efficiency (see, for example Monk Haller, 1986, Sher Tompkins, 1977, Walberg Fowler, 1987). At the same time, and as we noted previously other research suggests that small schools have important social and educational advantages.

This massive reform of U.S. education was carried our over the sometimes fierce resistance of parents and small communities. Indeed, the consolidation of small rural schools in this country belies the notion that strong community support is essential for substantial educational change to occur. District consolidations were often achieved in fractious, tempestuous conflict that pitted a small number of professional educators and their allies against large segments of local communities (see, for example, Monk $ Haller, 1986; Peshkin,1982; Tyack,1974, Weaver, 1977). The frequency with which the educators won these battles (as the statistics on the declining numbers of districts attest) is remarkable,.

The last big wave of rural school consolidations took place during the 1960s. In that decade the number of school districts in the United States was halved, and the one-teacher elementary schools virtually disappeared (National Center for Education Statistics,

1982). By the 1970s district consolidations had slowed to a trickle. In New York, for example, mergers occurred on the average of 20 per year between 1963 and 1967. A decade later they were a averaging one per year (Monk $ Haller, 1986).

It is important to note that this decline did not result simply because there were not small districts left. Today in New York there are 723 K-12 school districts. Two hundred and forty-five (33 percent) serve fewer than 1,000 pupils, 120 (17 percent) fewer than 500, and 41 (6 percent) fewer than 200. Rather, many districts *chose* to remain small. This is a sometimes bitter, protected struggles (Woodward, 1986) they successfully resisted the efforts of educators and state officials to merge them with their neighbors.

Educators who now hold positions of authority in local educational authorities (LEAs) and on state educational bureaucracies began their administrative careers during these "school wars" They received their administrative training during the 1950s and 1960s, when educational research, administration texts and such influential books as Conant's *The American High School* (1959) were uniformly praising large size. Their training, their successes in the 1960s and their subsequent failures have indelibly marked their views of rural schools. These experiences will influence their strategies for implementing current reforms in this country's hinterlands.

Evidence for this prediction comes from our study of the effects of school district consolidation in New York (Monk & Haller, 1986,) which included interviews with school administration superintendents of intermediate-level school districts (who are state education department officials), and officeholders in the state education department, among numerous others. Ignorant of two decades of research, the large majority of these officials continue to attribute high levels of inequality and inefficiency to small districts and to claim these result from their small size. (Davis,1986:60). As just one example in 1981 after evidence contraindicating consolidation had been accumulating for years, one state official wrote concerning New York's earlier efforts to merge districts:

> I am sure that there are many who felt the school districts were being pushed too fast and too far [into consolidation]. But in truth it was too slow and not far enough; and the great majority of school districts in New York State are still too small to adequately function in our present society. Their size, or rather their lack of it, inhibits the school's flexibility to solve the difficult problems they currently face.... Continuing such a school system is a luxury we cannot afford is difficult to justify. (Framer, 1981, quoted in Davis,1986:47)

Further, their experience with school consolidations has New York officials with the firm conviction that rural residents resist mergers because they do not understand the benefits that will accrue to their children. Their resulting perception is that consolidation must be *sold* to a skeptical and ignorant public. In New York this selling takes various forms. State education department officials visit small districts and speak to citizens and board members about the advantages of consolidation, but not its disadvantages. The state has published various pamphlets on the virtues of consolidation and distributed these to LEAs. It will underwrite the cost of a study of consolidation's possibilities. And it is willing to send experts to a community to help organize a campaign to promote a merger.

The selling of consolidations in New York also takes less straightforward guises. For example, a district consolidation must be preceded by a study to evaluate its merits. These studies are carried out by hired consultants, nearly always current or retired state officials. We have found no studies that recommended against consolidation. In fact, few even suggested that there were any disadvantages to a merger. Certainly, the authors of these studies never mentioned to community residents or to the school boards that hired them that there was an extensive body of research that was highly equivocal about any improvements district consolidation might have on equality or efficiency.

What was notable about these various activities was not so much that state officials engage in various selling tactics to convince rural people to consolidate their schools nor that this selling often took on a decidedly disingenuous cast. Rather, what best illustrates how deeply ingrained is this commitment to consolidation is the fact that many did not see these activities as "selling" at all. In fact, some took considerable umbrage at this suggestion, viewing their one-sided presentations as "educating" relatively ignorant people about the desirability of abandoning their local school district.

Another notable aspect of officials 'views was their understanding of residents' motives for resisting school consolidation. Besides ignorance, we were frequently told that people oppose consolidations for capricious reasons. For example, old athletic rivalries, jealousies between communities, unwillingness to locate a new school in another town, and of course the "If it was good enough for me, it's good enough for my kids" rationale were all cited as the "real" reasons that people resist a reform that is in their own interest.

Finally, resistance was sometimes attributed to illegitimate motives. Consider these comments about school board members.

> [There] are two types of men and women who serve on school boards, without pay. One type is the altruistic person who serves without any selfish motive and whose main objective is to improve the program of the school. The other type is that person who has power and likes power and doesn't always put the needs of pupils first. He or she can be tempted to keep the status quo [i.e., to resist a consolidation] for a variety of reasons even including protection of friends or relatives who work for the school district. (Davis,1986:86)

At times this attribution of capricious and illegitimate motives promotes a profoundly antidemocratic attitude among these officials. Some clearly believed that, since rural people refuse to do what is patently right for their own children, they need to be forced to do what officials know to be right. Consider these comments:

> All small districts... should be eliminated, if need be by the [state] Commissioner's offices. They are and have been expensive, inefficient and indefensible in this day.

> [L]legislation is the only answer. Albany, in conjunction with the District Superintendents, should decide which schools are too small to operate efficiently. Legislation should be enacted that would greatly reduce aid for the inefficient. Then only those who could afford it would want to or should be able to remain small. (Davis,1986:63-64)

The first person believes that all expensive and inefficient" districts should be dissolved by an appointed official, regardless of residents' wishes. The latter person has an even more remarkable view. He believes that wealthy districts should be permitted to remain small. Poor ones should ne starved into submission.

The continuing push to consolidate small rural schools does not depend simply on the attitudes of aging state bureaucrats. The probability of school consolidations is substantially enhanced because powerful legal and structural mechanisms supporting reorganization are in place. These are the relics of the push to abolish small rural districts several decades ago. For example, New York provides very large financial incentives for districts to merge. It can also withhold aid for building construction from districts identified in a state document as too small. Further, when two or more districts decide to hold a referendum on a proposed merger, as the law requires the same law mandates that the ballots of residents in all concerned districts be mingled and then counted. Thus, a large majority of the residents of a relatively small community can oppose a consolidation, yet find their district merged with a larger neighbvour. Finally, it is very important to note that in New York's State Education Department there is a Bureau of School District Organization. One of this bureau's major functions is to monitor school consolidations and to administer the procedures that govern them. But monitoring and administering, obviously, require that consolidations occur. Thus, a state agency and its associated officials have a vested interest in insuring that district mergers regularly take place.

We conclude that in New York State a reform movement of historical proportions, district consolidation, has become thoroughly institutionalized. Supporting belief systems, legal authority, and social structures are all deeply rooted in the state's educational landscape. The modern reform movement, then is laid on top of this legacy of earlier reform and, we believe, will be shaped by it.

But our data derive from only one state. We do not know the extent to which New York's experience differs from that of others. Undoubtedly it does in many respects. Nevertheless, and as we shall show, there is reason to believe that the consolidation movement has been institutionalized in other states as well—and with the same consequences for current reform efforts.

The Future Of Small Rural Schools

We can now draw conclusions about the modern reform movement's likely impact on small rural school districts. There are two points to make. On the one hand, there is an unmistakable congruence between the long standing effort to consolidate small rural schools and the hard dimension of the current schools improvement effort, with its emphasis on enhanced academic offerings and accountability. Officials in state education departments across the land can be expected to resonate to these calls for improved, cost-efficient programs. It is an old and reassuring refrain to the ears of those in positions of power.

On the other hand, there is no comparable congruence between the consolidation movement and the "soft" side of the modern reform effort, with its emphasis on the social development of youth, keeping schools close to their communities, increased parent involvement, and decentralized decision-making. These are new to the landscape of state education officials, and there is no tradition into which they comfortably fit. Indeed, these ideas are in many respects antithetical to some of their more cherished beliefs.

Moreover, there is the matter of cost. As states proceed to increase graduation requirements, the poorest and the smallest districts with the most minimal programs will face the greatest strain. This strain may persuade residents in these districts to believe assertions that consolidation will reduce school costs, especially when those assertions are made by "experts" who fail to cite contradictory evidence. Further, residents' willingness to accept reorganization as a solution to their fiscal problems will be accentuated by the large fiscal incentives offered for district mergers. (In New York these typically amount to several million dollars of additional state aid awarded over a period of fifteen years.) Thus, the modern, reform movement is likely to prompt additional school district reorganization efforts, despite its virtual silence on the question of size and its concern for social development of youth, parent involvement and decentralized decision-making.

Much of what we have said is speculative and based on research in one state. Nevertheless, it is worth nothing that recently at least eight states (Georgia, Illinois, Iowa, Massachusetts, New York North Carolina, Utah, and Vermont) have evidenced renewed efforts to consolidate their small school districts. Our analysis suggests that this renewed interest has come about, at least in part, because the seeds of hard reform have fallen on fertile ground is state education bureaucracies.

This suggestion is supported by additional evidence. As our analysis would predict, these renewed efforts spring from state-level sources. For example, in Illinois an executive branch initiative prompted a state department study recommending further consolidation (Illinois State Board of Education 1985,). North Carolina's efforts followed a similar course (North Carolina Department of Public Instruction, 1986). In New York and at state education department's behest, the legislature has made available 'efficiency study grants" of up to $20,000 to two or more districts willing to study cooperatively the possibilities of consolidating or otherwise sharing programs. (It is worth nothing that even the title of this program implies that enlarging school districts promotes efficiency.) Our own study of reorganization in New York was prompted by small districts' concerns over what the Regents Action Plan (New York's "hard" side or reform) would mean for their future. In Vermont, the governor appointed as Special Commission on Public School Governance, which called for further consolidation of Vermont schools in October 1987.

Moreover, state-level officials continue to ignore the large body of research that questions the wisdom of creating larger school districts. In 1986 in North Carolina, officials of the state education department prepared a document urging a sweeping, mandated reorganization of the state's school, creating one district per county. These officials concluded that "recent research" showed that North Carolina's school districts should serve at least 5,000 students each and that the optimal number was 10,000. As Sher (1986) points out in a scathing critique, the authors of this report relied on no research conducted after 1971; and, like their New York counterparts, they failed even to mention studies (one conducted by a member of their own department) that questioned the value of large size. Sher also found, as we did, that when these officials conducted studies of the feasibility of specific consolidations, they *always* found in favor of the proposed merger.

Thus, the sudden reawakening of interest in consolidation among state education officials is no accident. It stems from the compatibility of hard reforms with old and deeply embedded ideas about the virtues of large schools. In addition, the mechanisms for consolidation are in place in many states, and consolidation is a familiar tool for "improving" small rural schools. To paraphrase an old adage, " When your favorite tool is a hammer every problem is a nail".

Perhaps most fundamentally the renewed interest in consolidation may be another example of the common political phenomenon we noted in the beginning of this chapter. We have seen numerous examples of the power of local, state, and federal agencies to "capture" a public policy, especially a policy aimed at reforming the agency itself or the enterprise it is supposed to oversee. In this process, public policy can be transformed to serve the agencies' own ends, sometimes in ways contrary to the intentions of the reformers who proposed an idea and the legislative body that codified that idea into law (Harrigan, 1976; Stone, Whelan, & Murin, 1986). Indeed, we have seen examples of this phenomenon in education (Rodgers, 1969, Zeigler Tucker, & Wilson 1976).

It will be unfortunate if the current reform effort is captured by state bureaucrats and used for a largely discredited purpose, the further consolidation of small rural schools. Few current reformers have given much thought to the implications of their recommendations for the issue of schools size. Those who have thought about size do not view large schools as a desirable goal. We suspect that this is also true of those who are mute on the matter. Further, while the effect of school size on many educational outcomes is problematic, it is least so in regard to reform soft objectives. That is large, complex, and bureaucratized schools are inimical to the social and moral goals sought by reformers. It would be a bitter irony, then were a successful reform movement to spawn in the nation's small rural schools some of the very pathologies that the reformers were seeking to cure.

10

Reform of Problem Teachers

Poor performance is a problem facing all organizations and all professions, including the teaching profession. In a study of the Fortune 500 companies, the flagships of American business and industry, 97 percent of the administrators responding to a recent survey indicated that they were currently supervising an ineffective subordinate (Stoeberl & Schniederjans, 1981). This problem is felt at all levels of management in these companies and is on the increase. Doctors and lawyers, as well as industrial chiefs, have incompetents in their midst. Malpractice suits plague the medical profession (King, 1977), and lawyers are charged with ineffectively representing their clients (Burger, 1968; Finer, 1973). Poor performers are also to be found in the nation's classrooms, and the number of students who are being taught by these ineffective teachers exceeds the total combined public school enrollments of our 14 smallest states (Bridges, 1986). Clearly, incompetence is a pervasive and serious problem.

Educational reformers, whether from the first or the second wave, offer solutions to this problem that reflect little, if any, first-hand understanding of the realities of the workplace. These reformers are oblivious to the universal nature of the problem and are ignorant of how educational administrators actually deal with poor performers. Accordingly, the recommendations of these reformers rest more on conviction and philosophical persuasion than on a careful study of what is happening and why.

Unlike those of these first- and second-wave reformers, my

diagnosis and prescription are based on a five-year study of how school administrators actually deal with the problem of poor performance in the classroom. Morecver, my treatment of the problem centers on the inner workings of local school districts and attempts to reach a level of concreteness generally missing in both the first and the second wave of educational reforms.

With this context in mind, let us now examine in somewhat greater detail how administrators in educational institutions deal with ineffective teachers. Managerial responses fall into two general classes: *tolerance,* the more common response, and *confrontation.* Within each class there are several different responses to the poor performer; these various responses are arrayed along the continuum depicted in Figure 28.1. As we shall see, these managerial responses seldom lead to improvement in the ineffective teacher's performance; the underlying reasons for this lack of improvement suggest an organizational response that offers the possibility for greater success.

Tolerating the Poor Performer

School administrators exhibit their inclination to tolerate the ineffective teacher's performance in five ways. They may *ignore* what is happening by looking the other way or by convincing themselves that the problem is not really that serious. Alternatively, administrators may *complain* to significant others (e.g., friends, colleagues, or superiors) that the teacher really does not belong in the classroom; griping becomes a substitute for forthright action. Despite the complaints and the recognition that a problem exists, the administrator may *inflate the rating* of the poor performer in the mistaken belief that this action will act as positive reinforcement and thereby improve the teacher's performance. When this response fails, the administrator begins to *equivocate* by using double-talk, a form of verbal Novocaine, to deaden the sting of criticism.

The discussion of "Tolerating the Poor Performer" is a summary of the research reported in *The Incompetent Teacher* (Bridges, 1986).

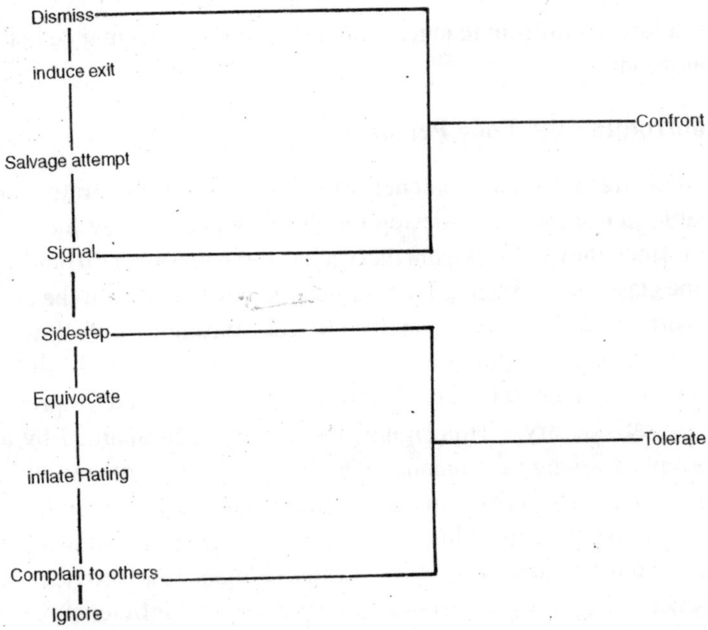

Figure 10. Steps in Tolerating and Confronting the Poor Performer.

If the problem persists and parents start to complain vehemently about what is happening to their children, administrators seek ways to *sidestep* the problems created by these parental complaints (Bridges, 1986). In an effort to skirt these problems and to shield the teacher from parental criticism, school administrators use several types of escape hatches. Transferring the teacher to another school is a favorite escape hatch. When trying to find a new home for the poor performer, administrators look for schools where parents are unlikely to complain, schools attended by minority children and those of low socioeconomic status. School administrators refer to this practice as "the dance of the lemons." Another escape hatch is a teaching assignment that removes the teacher from continuing contact with the same group of students (e.g., as a roving substitute or a member of the home-teaching staff). A third type of escape hatch entails reassignment of the poor performer to a nonteaching position (e.g., school bus driver, custodian, or clerk). Sidestepping, ignoring, complaining, inflating evaluations, and equivocating all represent tolerant responses because they share a common feature

— failure to confront teachers about their poor performance in the classroom.

Confronting the Poor Performer

If these various escape hatches are closed and administrators are unable to use them to sidestep the problems created by the poor performer, they will confront the teacher about his or her difficulties in the classroom. When administrators decide to confront the poor performer, their actions usually progress through the following stages (Bridges, 1986). First, the administrator *signals* that a problem exists by formally issuing a rating of "needs to improve" or "unsatisfactory." This signal is generally accompanied by an attempt to *salvage* the teacher. These salvage attempts involve a period of unmated criticism, where straight talk replaces double talk and equivocation. In addition, the administrator spells out what the teacher must do to improve his or her performance and provides the teacher with limited assistance to overcome the deficiencies that have been noted. This assistance typically includes opportunities to visit the classes of exceptional teachers and to attend workshops on a variety of topics, such as assertive discipline.

When the salvage attempt fails, administrators turn their attention to how to get rid of the poor performer. The way administrators choose to attain this goal depends on the employment status of the teacher. If the teacher has tenure, what the Chinese call the "iron rice bowl," administrators are inclined to *induce* the teacher to resign or to request an early retirement.

These induced exits typically involve four distinctive actions by administrators (Bridges, 1986). First, they exert a great deal of pressure on the teacher by increasing the flow of negative communications, using threat and intimidation, issuing formal notices of deficiency, and declaring the intention to institute dismissal proceedings if the teacher does not improve his or her performance. Second, the administrator negotiates with the teacher in an effort to learn what obstacles stand in the way of the teacher's departure and to reach agreement about the terms of the separation. Third, the administrator works behind the scenes to secure the cooperation of the teacher's union in persuading the teacher to leave quietly. This cooperation is forthcoming only after the union has become convinced that the teacher is incompetent and has been treated fairly by the administration. Fourth, the administration offers inducements to the poor performer in exchange for his or her resignation or early retirement. These inducements commonly include one or more of the following: medical coverage for a fixed period of time, employment in the district as a consultant for a period up to five years, a cash settlement, employment as a substitute teacher in the district for 30 to 45 days per year, and paid leave for the remainder of the school year.

If the administration fails to induce the exit or the teacher has probationary status and is not entitled to due process, administrators move toward dismissal. This is an extremely rare event. For example, in the state of California fewer than 0.6 percent of the teachers who were dismissed for incompetence over the two-year period spanning September 1, 1982, through the spring of 1984. The vast majority of the teachers who were dismissed did not have tenure. Tenured teachers, by a margin of 20 to 1, were induced to resign, not dismissed.

Responses of the Poor Performer

How the poor-performing teacher responds to the administrator depends to a large extent on the way in which the administrator chooses to deal with the problem of poor performance. If the administrator tolerates the substandard performance by ignoring the problem, complaining about it, inflating the poor performer's ratings, or equivocating, the teacher *ignores the problem* simply because he or she believes there is no problem. If administrators decide to sidestep the problem when parental complaints surface, the teacher typically *gripes* about the new assignment and exhibits similar performance problems in a different setting.

When the administrator begins to confront the problem, the teacher reacts quite strongly. Criticism initially begets *denial* that a problem exists. Teachers who finally acknowledge that they are having difficulties *blame* them on circumstances beyond their control—students who do not care, impossible working conditions, and uncooperative parents. In the face of continued criticism, the teacher may *attack* the source of the criticism and accuse administrators of unprofessional conduct, unfairness, and having unreasonable expectations. At the point where the administrator undertakes a salvage attempt, specifies what the teacher should be doing to improve, and prescribes assistance, the teacher's poor performance *persists.* If improvement occurs, it is hardly dramatic, simply enough to avert dismissal for incompetence.

When the teacher's performance fails to improve, the administrator presses for an induced exit or dismissal. Teachers under fire generally *leave;* however, their reactions to what is happening vary. Some are angry and embittered while others are relieved and even grateful for having been extricated from a painful situation. Their reactions depend to an extent on whether they perceive that the administration has made a good-faith attempt to provide assistance and treated them with dignity during the process. As we have seen, relatively few teachers are likely to experience such reactions because fewer than 1 percent a year are dismissed or induced to leave. The net result is a substandard education for more than two million students each year.

The Diagnosis and a Possible Cure

The preceding analysis highlights several major problems. One is the reluctance of administrators to confront poor-performing teachers unless there are numerous complaints from parents, while another is the failure of teachers to improve much, if any, even when they are confronted. Conceivably, both problems stem from the same root the unwillingness of individuals, whether administrators or teachers, to own the problem and to acknowledge partial, if not full, responsibility for doing something constructive about it. Both parties go to great lengths to find reasons for doing little, if anything, to solve the problem. The cure for this underlying ailment may lie in creating conditions within school organizations that are conducive to admitting that a problem exists and assuming responsibility for solving it.

A starting point for creating these conditions is to define norms within the organization that explicitly underscore the importance of "personal responsibility as the key to professional growth through evaluation." A set of norms that are congruent with this view should be reflected in the philosophy of evaluation and the associated operating procedures. The following example illustrates how the norms of personal responsibility as a key to professional growth through evaluation can be institutionalized within an educational organization.

Philosophy of Teacher Evaluation

Teaching is a noble, but demanding, occupation. In order for teachers to maintain a high level of professional performance under these conditions, they must assume personal responsibility for their own performance, growth, and development. The exercise of this responsibility is admittedly difficult and is likely to occur only when administrators exhibit genuine concern for the teacher's welfare and facilitate the teacher's effort to assume personal responsibility. In those rare instances when an overriding concern for the teacher's welfare runs contrary to the best interests of the school and the students, administrators will assume the responsibility if the teacher is unable or unwilling to do so.

Policies and Procedures

Teacher evaluation is to be implemented in two distinct stages.

Stage 1

During this stage no teacher, except under grossly unusual circumstances, will receive a negative evaluation or a needs-to-improve designation. Moreover, during stage 1 no written record will be kept of what has transpired; the responsibilities of administrators and teachers during this period are as follows.

Administrators. In this stage the administrator is to function as an ally who nudges teachers and facilitates their efforts to assume personal responsibility for their own professional performance, growth, and development. More specifically:

1. The administrator *nudges* by calling problems that the teacher may be having, but may not be recognizing, to the teacher's attention in a casual but friendly manner and offering whatever assistance the teacher deems useful or necessary.
2. The administrator *facilitates* by providing assistance whenever it is feasible to do so. This assistance may take a variety of forms, including (a) altering the teacher's working conditions, (b) providing access to individuals who are capable and interested in working with the teacher, (c) supplying access to personal counseling for dealing with crisis situations and personal problems, and (d) providing access to therapy for treating specific disorders like alcoholism or drug abuse.

Teachers. During stage 1 the teacher is expected to respond as someone would to an individual who is perceived to be acting in the teacher's best interests. Specifically:

1. The teacher should acknowledge that he or she has a problem for which he or she is fully or partially responsible, to accept the responsibility for (a) understanding what the nature of the problem is; (b) figuring out why it may be occurring; and (c) deciding what should be done to eliminate the problem including what assistance is desired.
2. The teacher should face reality that is, confront the possibility that the problem may or may not have been satisfactorily resolved; that the problem, if not resolved, may be serious enough to raise doubts about the wisdom of the teacher's decision to be a teacher; and that the course of action that may be in the best interests of the teacher and the district is for the teacher to pursue another line of work with assistance from the district.

Stage 2

If the problem persists and the situation seriously impairs the school and/or the students, the administrator will assume primary responsibility for dealing with the teachers's problem. However, before entering this stage, the administrator will indicate to the teacher that he or she seems to have reached the point where the teacher must make a choice. Should the teacher be given one more opportunity to exercise responsibility for solving the problem, or should the administrator become more directive in attempting to resolve it? If the teacher chooses to forego the opportunity, the administrator will do one or more of the following in sequential order as the situation warrants: (a) issue a needs-to-improve and/or an unsatisfactory evaluation of the teacher's performance; (b) prescribe a program of remediation; (c) evaluate the teacher to see if sufficient improvement has occurred to warrant continued employment in the district as a teacher; (d) issue a notice of the intent to dismiss if the person does not improve within a specified period of time; and (e) recommend dismissal if the person fails to improve.

Conclusion

The responses to unsatisfactory performance in elementary and secondary schools are ineffective. Managers typically tolerate the poor performance. The poor performers, even when they are confronted, rarely improve; if they do, their performance remains marginal at best. Underlying the in effective responses of both teachers and administrators is the unwillingness to own the problem and to assume responsibility for solving it. If administrators are to oversome their reluctance to let teachers know when they are in difficulty, and if teachers are to own the problem and seek to solve it, new norms for teacher evaluation must be created. These norms should be grounded in the belief that "personal responsibility is the key to professional growth through evaluation."

On its surface the proposal seems to emphasize the teacher's, not the administrator's, personal responsibility. Such is not the case. Under this proposal, administrators, once they have called a problem to the attention of the teacher, must face the possibility that the teacher's difficulties are due to an unreasonable set of organizational demands, unfavourable working conditions, and insufficient resources. Moreover, the administrator has the responsibility to make a concerted effort to alter these factors. Implementation of a new philosophy and a set of operating procedures for carrying out teacher evaluation, such as the ones discussed in this proposal, will not be straightforward. As with any organizational change that entails a restructuring of beliefs and behavior, administrators will need to consult with teachers in seeking answers to questions like the following:

1. What conditions need to be present, which are not now, if these changes are to be implemented?
2. What obstacles stand in the way of these changes being implemented? How might we remove these obstacles?
3. If the new philosophy and set of operating procedures were implemented, what do we fear might happen? If these things did happen, how serious would they be? If they are serious, how might we prevent these unwelcome consequences from occurring?

The proper way of judging this proposal for restructuring teacher evaluation to promote personal responsibility is not whether it is flawless, but whether it produces more beneficial and less harmful consequences than current practices. Given the woeful state of what is now happening, the proposal warrants a trial. The risk is small, and the possibility for substantial rewards is great. The two million students who are being short-changed by the shopworn philosophy and practices of the past deserve a chance for a better fate.

11

Unequal Education

The ideological defense of modern capitalist society rests heavily on the assertion that the equalizing effects of education can counter the disequalizing forces inherent in the free market system. That educational systems in capitalist societies have been highly unequal is generally admitted and widely condemned. Yet educational inequalities are taken as passing phenomena, holdovers from an earlier, less enlightened era, which are rapidly being eliminated.

The record of educational history in the U.S., and scrutiny of the present state of our colleges and schools, lend little support to this comforting optimism. Rather, the available data suggest an alternative interpretation. In what follows I will argue 1) that schools have evolved in the U.S., not as part of a pursuit of equality, but rather to meet the needs of capitalist employers for a disciplined and skilled labor force, and to provide a mechanism for social control in the interests of-political stability; 2) that as the economic importance of skilled and well educated labor has grown, inequalities in the school system have become increasingly important in reproducing the class structure from one generation to the next; 3) that the U.S. school system is pervaded by class inequalities, which have shown little sign of diminishing over the last half century; and 4) that the evidently unequal control over school boards decision-making bodies in education does not provide a sufficient explanation of the persistence and pervasiveness of inequalities in the school system. Although the unequal distribution of political power serves to maintain inequalities in education, their origins are to be fond outside the political sphere, in the class structure itself and in the class subcultures typical of capitalist societies. Thus unequal education has its roots in the very class structure with it serves to legitimize and reproduce. Inequalities in education are thus seen as part of the web of capitalist society, and likely to persist as long as capitalism survives.

1. The Evolution Of Capitalism And The Rise Of Mass Education

In colonial America, and in most pre-capitalist societies of the past, the basic productive unit was the family. For the vast majority of male adults, work was self-directed, and was performed without direct supervision. Though constrained by poverty, ill health, the low level of technological development and occasional interferences by the political authorities, a man had considerable leeway in choosing his working hours, what to produce it. While great inequalities in wealth, political power, and other aspects of status normally existed, differences in the degree of autonomy in work were relatively minor, particularly when compared with what was to come.

Transmitting the necessary productive skills to the children as they grew up proved to be a simple task, not because the work was devoid of skill, but because the quite substantial skills required were virtually unchanging from generation to generation, and because the transition to the world of work did not require that the child adapt to a wholly new set of social relationships. The child learned the concrete skills and adapted to the social relations of production through learning by doing within the family. Preparation for life in the larger community was facilitated by the child's experience with the extended family, which shaded off without distinct boundaries, through uncles and fourth cousins, into the community. Children learned early how to deal with complex relationship among adults other than their parents, and children other than their brothers and sisters.

It was not required that children learn a complex set of political principles or ideologies, as political participation was limited and political authority unchallenged, at least in normal times. The only major socializing institution outside the family was the church, which sought to inculcate the accepted spiritual values and attitudes. In addition a small number of children learned craft skills outside the family, as apprentices. The role of schools tended to be narrowly vocational, restricted to preparation of children for a career in the church or the still inconsequential state bureaucracy. The curriculum of the few universities reflected the aristocratic penchant for conspicuous intellectual consumption.

The extension of capitalist production, and particularly the factory system, undermined the role of the family as the major unit of both socialization and production. Small peasant farmers were driven off the land or competed out of business. Cottage industry was destroyed. Ownership of the means of production became heavily concentrated in the hands of landlords and capitalists. Workers relinquished control over their labor in return for wages or salaries. Increasingly, production was carried on in large organizations in which a small management group directed the work activities of the entire labor force. The social relations of production—the authority structure, the prescribed types of behavior and response characteristic of the work place—became increasingly distinct form those of the family.

The divorce of the worker from control over production—from control over his own labor-is particularly important in understanding the role of schooling in capitalist societies. The resulting social division of labor—between controllers and controlled—is a crucial aspect of the class structure of capitalist societies, and will be seen to be an important barrier to the achievement of social class equality in schooling.

Rapid economic change in the capitalist period led to frequent shifts in the occupational distribution of the labor force, and constant changes in the skill requirements for jobs. The productive skills of the father were no longer adequate for the needs of the son during his lifetime. Skill training within the family became increasingly inappropriate.

And the family itself was changing. Increased geographic mobility of labor and the necessity for children to work outside the family spelled the demise of the extended family and greatly weakened even the nuclear family. Meanwhile, the authority of the church was questioned by the spread of secular rationalist thinking and the rise of powerful competing groups.

While undermining the main institutions of socialization, the development of the capitalist system created at the same time an environment—both social and intellectual—which would ultimately challenge the political order. Workers were thrown together in oppressive factories and the isolation which had helped to maintain quiescence in earlier, widely dispersed peasant populations was broken down. With an increasing number of families uprooted form the land, the workers' search for a living resulted in largescale labor migrations. Transient—even foreign—elements came to constitute a major segment of the population, and began to pose seemingly insurmountable problems of assimilation, integration and control. Inequalities of wealth became more apparent, and were less easily justified and less readily accepted. The simple legitimizing ideologies of the earlier period—the divine right of kings and the divine origin of social rank, for example—fell under the capitalist attack on the royalty and the traditional landed interests. The broadening of the electorate of political participation generally—first sought by the capitalist class in the struggle against the entrenched interests of the pre-capitalist period—threatened soon to become an instrument for the growing power of the working class. Having risen to political power, the capitalist class sought a mechanism to insure social control and political stability.

An institutional crisis was at hand. The outcome in virtually all capitalist countries, was the rise of mass education. In the U.S., the many advantages of schooling as a socialization process were quickly perceived. The early proponents of the rapid expansion of schooling argued that education could perform many of the socialization functions which earlier had been centered in the family and to a lesser extent, in the church.

An ideal preparation for factory work was found in the social relations of the school: specifically, in its emphasis on discipline, punctuality, acceptance of authority outside the family and individual accountability for one's work. The social relations of the school would replicate the social relations of the workplace, and thus help young people adapt to the social division of labor. Schools would further lead people to accept the authority of the state and its agents—the teachers—at a young age, in part by fostering the illusion of the benevolence of the government in its relations with citizens. Moreover, because schooling would ostensibly be open to all, one's position in the social division of labor could be portrayed as the result not of birth but of one's own efforts and talents. And if the children's everyday experiences with the structure of schooling were insufficient to inculcate the correct views and attitudes, the curriculum itself would be made to embody the bourgeois ideology. Where pre-capitalist social institutions—particularly the church-remained strong or threatened the capitalist hegemony, schools sometimes served as a modernizing counter-institution.

The movement for public elementary and secondary education in the U.S. originated in the 19th century in states dominated by the burgeoning industrial capitalist class, most notably in Massachusetts. It spread rapidly to all parts of the country except the South. In Massachusetts the extension of elementary education was in large measure a response to industrialization, and to the need for social control of the Irish and other non-Yankee workers recruited to work in the mills. The fact that some working people's movements had demanded free instruction should not obscure the basically coercive nature of the extension of schooling. In many parts of the country, schools were literally imposed upon the workers.

The evolution of the economy in the 19th century gave rise to new socialization needs and continued to spur the growth of education. Agriculture continued to lose ground to manufacturing; simple manufacturing gave way to production involving complex interrelated processes: an increasing fraction of the labor force was employed in producing services rather than goods. Employers in the most rapidly growing sectors of the economy began to require more than obedience and punctuality in their workers; a change in motivational outlook was required. The new structure of production provided little built-in motivation. There were fewer jobs like farming and piece-rate work in manufacturing in which material reward was tied directly to effort. As work roles became more complicated and interrelated, the evaluation of the individual worker's performance became increasingly difficult. Employers began to look for workers who had internalized the production-related values of the firm's managers.

The continued expansion of education was pressed by many who saw schooling as a means of producing these new forms of motivation and discipline. Others, frightened by the growing labor militancy after the Civil War, found new urgency in the social control arguments popular among the proponents of education in the antebellum period.

A system of class stratification development within this rapidly expanding educational system. Children of the social elite normally attended private schools. Because working class children tended to leave school early, the class composition of the public high schools was distinctly more elite than the public primary schools. And as a university education ceased to be merely training for teaching or the divinity and became important in gaining access to the pinnacles of the business world, upper class families used their money and influence to get their children into the best universities, often at the expense into the best universities, often at the expense of the children of less elite families.

Around the turn of the present century, large numbers of working class and particularly immigrant children began attending high schools. At the same time, a system of class stratification development within secondary education. The older democratic ideology of the common school—that the same curriculum should be offered to all children—gave way to the "progressive" insistence that education should be tailored to the "needs if the child." In the interests of providing an education relevant to the later life of the students, vocational schools and tracks were developed for the children of working families. The academic curriculum was preserved for those who would later have the opportunity to make use of book learning, either in college or in white-collar employment. This and other educational reforms of the progressive education movement reflected an implicit assumption of the immutability of the class structure.

The frankness with which students were channeled into curriculum tracks, on the basis of their social class background, raised serious doubts concerning the "openness" of the social class structure. The relation between social class and a child's chances of promotion or tracking assignments was disguised—though not mitigated much—by another "progressive" reform: "objective" educational testing. Particularly after World War I, the capitulation of the schools to business values and concepts of efficiency led to the increased use of intelligence and scholistic achievement testing as an ostensibly unbiased means of measuring the product of schooling and classifying students.

The complementary growth of the guidance counseling profession allowed much of the channeling to proceed from the students' own well-counseled choices, thus adding an apparent element of volutarism to the system.

The legacy of the progressive education movement, like the earlier reforms of the mid-19th century, was a strengthened system of class stratification within schooling which continues to this day to play an important role in the reproduction and legitimation of the social division of labor.

The class stratification of education during this period had proceeded hand in hand with the stratification of the labor force. As large bureaucratic corporations and public agencies employed an increasing fraction of all workers, a complicated segmentation of the labor force evolved, reflecting the hierarchical structure of the social relations of production. A large middle group of employees evolved comprising the clerical, sales, bookkeeping, and low level supervisory workers. People holding these occupations ordinarily had a modicum of control over their own work: in some cases they directed the work of others while themselves being under the direction of higher management. The social division of labor had become a finely articulated system of work relations dominated at the top by a small group with control over work processes and a high degree of personal autonomy in their work activities, and proceeding by finely differentiated stages down the chain of bureaucratic command to workers who labored more as extensions of the machinery than as autonomous human beings.

One's status, income, and personal autonomy came to depend in great measure on one's place in the hierarchy of work relations. And in turn, positions in the social division of labor came to be associated with educational credentials reflecting the number of years of schooling and the quality of education received. The increasing importance of schooling as a mechanism for allocating children to positions in the class structure, played a major part in legitimizing the structure itself. But at the same time, it undermined the simple processes which in the past had preserved the position and privilege of the upper class families from generation to generation. In short, it undermined the processes serving to reproduce the social division of labor.

In pre-capitalist societies, direct inheritance of occupational position is common. Even in the early capitalist economy, prior to the segmentation of the labor force on the basis of differential skills and education, the class structure was reproduced generation after generation simply through the inheritance of physical capital by the offspring of the capitalist class. Now that the social division of labor is differentiated by types of competence and educational credentials as well as by the ownership of capital, the problem of inheritance is not nearly as simple. The crucial complication arises because education and skills are embedded in human beings, and unlike physical capital—these assets cannot be passed on to one's children at death. In an advanced capitalist society in which education and skills play an important role in the hierarchy of production, then, the absence of confiscatory inheritance laws is not enough to reproduce the social division of labor from generation to generation. Skills and educational credentials must somehow be passed on within the family. It is a fundamental theme of this paper that schools play an important part in reproducing and legitimizing this modern form of class structure.

2. Class Inequalities In U.S. School

Unequal schooling reproduces the social division of labor. Children whose parents occupy positions at the top of the occupational hierarchy receive more years of schooling than working class children. Both the amount and the content of their education greatly facilitates their movement into positions similar to their movement into positions to their parents'.

Because of the relative ease of measurement inequalities in years of schooling are particularly evident. If we define social class standing by the income, occupation, and educational level of the parents, a child from the 90th percentile in the class distribution may expect on the average to achieve over four and a half more years of schooling than a child from the 10th percentile. As can be seen in Table 1, social class inequalities in the number of years of schooling received arise in part because a disproportionate number of children from poorer families don't complete high school. Table 2 indicates that these inequalities are exacerbated by social class inequalities in college attendance among those children who did graduate form high school: even among those who had graduated form high school, children of families earning less than $3,000 per year were over six times as likely not to attend college as were the children of families earning over $15,000.

Because schooling—especially at the college level is heavily subsidized by the general tax-payer, those children who attend school longer have access—for this reason alone-to a far larger amount of public resources than those who are forced out or drop out early. But social class inequalities in public expenditure on education are far more severe than the degree of inequality in years of schooling would suggest. In the fist place,-student public expenditure in four-year colleges greatly exceeds that in elementary schools; those who stay in school longer receive an increasingly large *annual* public subsidy. Second, even at the elementary level, schools attended by children of the poor tend to be less well-endowed with equipment, books, teachers, and other inputs into the educational process. Evidence on the relationship between the level of school inputs and the income of the neighborhoods which the schools serve is presented in Table 3. The data in this table indicate that both schools expenditures and more direct measures of school quality very directly with the income levels of the communities in which the school is located.

Table 1. Percentage of Male Children aged 16-17 Enrolled in Public School and Percentage at Less that the Modal Grade Level, by Parent's Education and Income, 1960[a]

	% of male children aged 16-17 enrolled in public school	%of those enrolled who are below the modal level
1.Parent's education less than 8 years		
Family Income:		
less than $3,000	66.1	47.4
$3,000-4,999	71.3	35.7
$5,000-6,999	75.5	28.3
$7,000 and over	71.1	21.8
2.Parent's education 8-11 years		
Family income:		
less than $3,000	78.6	25.0
$3,000-4,999	82.9	20.9
$5,000-6,999	84.9	16.9
$7,000 and over	86.1	13.0
*3. Parent's education 12 years or more		
Family income:		
less than $3,000	89.2	13.4
$3,000-4,999	90.7	12.4
$5,000-6,999	92.1	9.7
$7,000 and over	94.2	16.9

Source : Bureau of the Census, Census of Population, Vol.PC-(2)5A, Table 5.

According to Bureau of the Census definitions, for 16-year olds 9th or less and for 17-year olds 10th grade of less are below the modal level. Father's education is indicated if father's is present: otherwise mother's education is indicated.

Table 2. College Attendance in 1967 among High School Graduates, by Family Gnome [a]

Family income[b]	*Percent who did not attend college*
Total	*53.1*
under$3,000	80.2
$3,000 to $3,999	67.7
$4,000 to $5,999	63.7
$6,000 to $7,499	58.9
$10,000 to $14,999	38.7
$15,000 and over	13.3

a. Refers to individuals who were high school seniors in October 1965 and who subsequently graduated from high school.

Source: U.S. Department of Commerce, Bureau of the Census, Current Population, Report, Series P-20 No. 185,July 11, 1969, P.6 College attendance refers to both two and four-year institutions.

b. Family income for 12 months preceding October 1965.

Inequalities is schooling are not simply a matter of differences in years of schooling attained or in resources devoted to each students per year of schooling. Differences in the internal structure of schools themselves and in the content of schooling reflect the difference in the social class compositions of the student bodies. The social relations of the educational process ordinarily mirror the social relations of the work roles into which most students are likely to move. Differences in rules, expected modes of behavior, and opportunities for choice are most glaring when we compare levels of schooling. Note the wide range of choice over curriculum, life-style, and allocation of time afforded to college students, compared with the obedience and respect for authority expected in high school. Differentiation occurs also with each level of schooling. One needs only to compare the social relations of a junior college with those of an elite four-year college, or those of a working class high schools with those of a wealth suburban high school, for verification of this point.

Table 3. Inequalities in Elementary School Resources: Percent Difference in Resource Availability Associated with a One Percent Difference in Mean Neighborhood Family Income

Resource	*Within cities (1)*	*Between cities (2)*
1. Current real education expenditure per student	n.a	.73[B]
2. Average real elementary school teacher salary	.20[a]	.69[b]
3. Teacher-student ratio	.24[a]	n.a
4. Real expenditure per pupil on teacher salary	.43[a]	n.a
5. Verbal ability of teacher	.11[a]	1.20[a]

Sources:

a. John D. Owen, "An Empirical Analysis of Economic and Racial Bias in the Distribution of Educational Resources in Nine Large American Cities" (Center for the Study of Social Organization of Schools Johns, Hopkins University, 1969).

b. John D. Owen , "Towards a Public Employment Wage Theory: Some Econometric Evidence on Teacher Quality," *Industrial Labor Relations Review* (forthcoming,1972).

The different socialization patterns in schools attended by students of different social classes do not arise by accident. Rather, they stem from the fact that the educational objectives and expectations of both parents and teachers, and the responsiveness of students to various patterns of teaching and control, differ for students of different social classes. Further, class inequalities in school socialization patterns are reinforced by the very inequalities in financial resources documented above. The paucity of financial support for the education of children form working class families not only leaves more resources to be devoted to the children of those with commanding roles in the economy; it forces upon the teachers and school administrators in the working class schools a type of social relations which fairly closely mirrors that of the factory. Thus financial considerations in poorly supported working class schools militate against small intimate classes, against a multiplicity of elective courses and specialized teachers (except disciplinary personnel), and preclude the amounts of free time for the teachers and free space required for a more open, flexible educational environment. The lack of financial support all but requires that students be treated as raw materials on a production line; it places a high premium on obedience and punctuality; there are few opportunities for independent, creative work or individualized attention by teachers. The well-financed schools attended by the children of the rich can offer much greater opportunities for the development of the capacity for sustained independent work and the other characteristics required for adequate job performance in the upper levels of the occupational hierarchy.

While much of the inequality in U.S. education exists between schools, even within a given school different children receive different educations. Class stratification within schools is achieved through tracking, differential participation in extracurricular activities, and in the attitudes of teachers and particularly guidance personnel who expect working class children to do poorly, to terminate schooling early, and to end up in jobs similar to their parents.

Not surprisingly the results of schooling differ greatly for children different social classes. The differing educational objectives implicit in the social relations of schools attended by children of different social classes has already been mentioned. Less important but more easily measured are differences in scholastic achievement. If we measure the output of schooling by scores on nationally standardized achievement tests, children whose parents were themselves highly educated outperform the children of parents with less education by a wide margin. A recent study revealed, for example, that among white high school seniors, those whose parents were in the top education decile were on the average well over there grade levels ahead of those whose parents were in the bottom decile. While a good part of this discrepancy is the result of unequal treatment in school and unequal education resources, it will be suggested below that much of it is related to differences in the early socialization and home environment of the children.

Given the great social class differences in scholastic achievement, class inequalities in college attendance are to be expected. Thus one might be tempted to argue that the data in Table 2 are simply a reflection of unequal scholastic achievement in high school and do not reflect any *additional* social class in equalities peculiar to the process of college admission. This view, so comforting to the admissions personnel in our elite universities,

Table 4. Probability of College Entry for a Male who has Reached Grade 11[a]

		Socioeconomic quartiles[b]			
		Low			*High*
		1	2	3	4
Ability	Low 1	.06	.12	.13	.26
Quartiles[b]	2	.13	.15.	29	.36
	High 4	.48	.70	.73	.87

a. Based on a large sample of U.S. high school students as reported in John C. Flanagan and William W. Colley, Project *TALENT, One-Year Follow-up Studies*, Cooperative Research Project Number 2333, School of Education, University of Pittsburgh, 1966.

b. The socioeconomic index is a composite measure including family income, father's occupation and education, mother's education, etc. The ability scale is a composite of tests measuring general academic aptitude is unsupported by the available data, some of which are presented in Table 4. Access to a college education is highly unequal, even for children of the same measured "academic ability."

The social class inequalities in our school system and the role they play in the reproduction of the social division of labor are too evident to be denied. Defenders of the educational system are forced back on the assertion that things are getting better; the inequalities of the past were far worse. And, indeed, there can be no doubt that some of the inequalities of the past have been mitigated. Yet new inequalities have apparently developed to take their place, for the available historical evidence lends little support to the idea that our schools are on the road to equality of educational opportunity. For example, data from a recent U.S. Census survey reported in Table 5 indicate that graduation from college has become increasingly dependent on one's class background. This is true despite the fact that the probability of high school graduation is becoming increasingly equal across social classes. On balance, the available data suggest that the number of years of schooling attained by a child depends upon the social class standing on the father at least as much in the recent period as it did fifty years ago.

The argument that our "egalitarian" education compensates for inequalities generated elsewhere in the capitalist system is so patently fallacious that few will persist in maintaining it. But the discrepancy between the ideology and the reality of the U.S school system is far greater than would appear from a passing glance at the above data. In the first place, if education is to compensate for the social class immobility due to the inheritance of wealth and privilege, education must be structured so as to yield a negative correlation between social class background of the child and the quantity and quality of her or his schooling. Thus the assertion that education compensates for inequalities in inherited wealth and privilege is falsified not so much by the extent of the social class inequalities in the school system as by their very existence, or, more correctly, by the absence of compensatory inequalities.

Table 5. Among Sons who had Reached High School, Percentage who graduated from college, by Son's Age And Father's Level of Education

			Father's education					
			Some high school		*High school grad*		*Some college or more*	
Son's age in 1962	*Likely dates of college graduation*[a]	*<8years*	*%* *Graduating*	*Ratio to<8*	*%* *Grad*	*Ratio to<8*	% Grad	Ratio to < 8
25–34	1950–1959	07.6	17.4	2.29	25.6	3.37	51.9	6.83
35–44	1940–1949	08.6	11.9	0.38	25.3	2.94	53.9	6.27
45–54	1930–1939	07.7	09.8	1.27	15.1	1.96	36.9	4.79
55–64	1920–1929	08.9	09.8	0.10	19.2	2.16	29.8	3.35

a. Assuming college graduation at age 22.

Source: Based on U.S. Census data as reported in William G. Spady, "Educational Mobility and Access: Growth and Paradoxes," *American Journal of Sociology, Vol.73, No.3 (November 1967).*

Second, if we turn now from the problem of intergeneration immobility to the problem of inequality of income at a given moment, a similar argument applies. In a capitalist economy, the increasing importance of schooling in the economy will exercise a disequalizing tendency on the distribution of income even in the absence of social class inequalities in quality and quantity of schooling. To see why this is so, consider a simple capitalist economy in which only two factors are used in production: uneducated and undifferentiated labor, and capital, the ownership of which is unequally distributed among the population. The only source of income inequality in this society is the unequal distribution of capital. As the labor force becomes differentiated by type of skill or schooling, inequalities in labor earnings contribute to total income inequality, augmenting the inequalities due to the concentration of capital. This will be the case even if education and skills are distributed randomly among the population. The disequalizing tendency will of course be intensified if the owners of capital also acquire a disproportionate amount of those types of education and training which confer access to high-paying jobs. A substantial negative correlation between the ownership of capital and the quality and quantity of schooling received would have been required merely to neutralize the disequalizing effect of the rise of schooling as an economic phenomenon. And while some research has minimized the importance of social class biases in schooling, nobody has yet suggested that class and schooling were inversely related!

3. Class Culture And Class Power

The pervasive and persistent inequalities in U.S. education would seem to refute an interpretation of education which asserts its egalitarian functions. But the facts of inequality do not by themselves suggest an alternate explanation. Indeed, they pose serious problems of interpretation. If the costs of education borne by students and their families were very high, or if nepotism were rampant, or if formal segregation of pupils by social class were practiced, or educational decisions were made by a select few whom we might call the power elite, it would not be difficult to explain the continued inequalities U.S. education. The problem of interpretation, however, is to reconcile the above empirical findings with the facts of our society as we perceive them: public and virtually tuition-free education at all levels, few legal instruments for the direct implementation of class segregation, a limited role for "contacts" or nepotism in the achievement of high status or income, a commitment (at the rhetorical level at least) to equality of educational opportunity, and a system of control of education which if not particularly democratic, extends far beyond anything resembling a power elite. The attempt to reconcile these apparently discrepant facts leads us back to a consideration of the social division of labor, the associated class cultures, and the exercise of class power.

I will argue that the social division of labor-based on the hierarchical structure of production—gives rise to distinct class subcultures. The values, personality traits and expectations characteristic of each subculture are transmitted from generation to generation through class differences in family socialization and complementary differences in the type and amount of schooling ordinarily attained by children of various class positions. These class differences in schooling are maintained in large measure through the capacity of the upper class to control the basic principles of school finance, pupil, evaluation and educational objectives.

This outline, and what follows, is put forward as an interpretation, consistent where testable with the available data, though lacking as yet in firm empirical support for some important links in the argument.

The social relations of production characteristic of advanced capitalist societies (and many socialist societies) are most clearly illustrated in the bureaucracy and hierarchy of the modern corporation. Occupational roles in the capitalist economy may be grouped according to the degree of independence and control exercised by the person holding the job. There is some evidence that the personality attributes associated with the adequate performance of jobs in occupational categories defined in this broad way differ considerably, some apparently requiring independence and internal discipline, and others emphasizing such traits as obedience, predictability and willingness to subject oneself to external controls.

These personality attributes are developed primarily at a young age, both in the family and to a lesser extent, in secondary socializing institutions such as schools. Because people tend to marry within their own class (in part because spouses often meet in our class segregated schools), both parents are likely to have a similar set of these fundamental personality traits. Thus children of parents occupying a given position in the occupational hierarchy grow up in homes where child-rearing methods and perhaps even the physical surroundings tend to develop personality characteristics appropriate to adequate job performance in the occupational roles of the parents. The children of managers and professionals are taught self-reliance within a broad set of constraints; the children of production line workers ate taught obedience.

While this relation between parents class position and child's personality attributes operates primarily in the home, it is reinforced by schools and other social institutions. Thus to take an example introduced earlier the authoritarian social relations of working class high schools complement the discipline-oriented early socialization patterns experienced by working class children. The relatively greater freedom of wealthy suburban schools extends and formalizes the early independence training characteristic of upper class families.

Schools reinforce other aspects family socialization as well. Student's and parents' aspirations and expectations concerning both the type and the amount of schooling are strongly related to social class. The expectations of teachers guidance counselors, and school administrators ordinarily reinforce those of the students and parents. Schools often encourage students to develop aspiration and expectations typical of their social class, even if the child tends to have "deviant" aspirations.

It is true to some extent schools introduce common elements of socialization for all students regardless of social class. Discipline, respect for property competition, and punctuality are part of the implicit curriculum of virtually all schools. Yet given the existing institutional arrangements, the ability of a school to change a child's personality, values, and expectations is severely limited. The responsiveness of children to different types of schooling seems to depend importantly upon the types of personality traits, values, and expectations which have been developed through the family. Furthermore children spend a small amount of time in school—less than a quarter of their waking hours over the course of a year. Thus schools are probably more effective where they attempt to complement and reinforce rather than to oppose the socialization processes of the home and neighborhood. It is not surprising, then, that social class differences in scholistic achievement and other measures of school success are far greater than would be accounted for by differences in the measured school financial resources and other inputs (quality and quantity of teachers etc.) alone.

Class differences in the total effect of schooling are—in this interpretation —due primarily to differences in what I have called class subculture. The educational system serves less to change the results of the primary socialization in the home than to ratify them and render them in adult form. The complementary relationship between family socialization and schools serves to reproduce patterns of class culture from generation to generation.

The operation of the labor market translates differences in class culture into income inequalities and occupational hierarchies. The personality traits, values, and expectations characteristic of different class cultures play a major role in determining an individual's success gaining a high income or prestigious occupation. The apparent contribution of schooling to occupational success and higher income seems to be explained primarily by the personality characteristics of those who have higher educational attainments. Although the rewards to intellectual capacities are quite limited in the labor market (except for a small number of high level jobs,) mental abilities are important in getting ahead in school. Grades, the probability of continuing to higher levels of schooling, and a host of other school success variables are positively correlated with "objective" measures of intellectual capacities. Partly for this reason, one's experience in school reinforces the belief that promotion and rewards are distributed fairly. The close relationship between educational attainments and later occupational success thus provides a meritocratic appearance to mask the mechanisms which reproduce the class system from generation to generation.

So far, the perpetuation of inequality through the schooling system has been represented as an almost automatic self-enforcing mechanism, operating only through the medium of class culture. An important further dimension of the interpretation is added if we note that positions of control in the productive hierarchy tend to be associated with positions of political influences. Given the disproportionate share of political power held by the upper class and their capacity to determine the accepted patterns of behavior and procedures, to define the national interest, and in general to control the ideological and institutional context in which educational decisions are made, it is not surprising to find that resources are allocated unequally among school tracks, between schools serving different classes, and between levels of schooling. The same configuration of power results in curricula, methods of instruction, and criteria of selection and promotion which confer benefits disproportionately on the children of the upper class.

It is not asserted here that the upper class controls the main decision-making bodies in education, although a good case could probably be made that this is so. The power of the upper class is hypothesized as existing in its capacity to define and maintain a set of rules of operation or decision criteri—''rules of the game" - which, though often seemingly innocuous and sometimes even egalitarian in their ostensible intent, have the effect of maintaining the unequal system.

The operation of two prominent examples of these "rules of the game" will serve to illustrate the point. The first important principle is that excellence in schooling should be rewarded. Given the capacity of the upper class to define excellence in terms on which upper class children tend to excel (for example scholastic achievement), adherence to this principle yields inegalitarian outcomes (for example, unequal access to higher education) while maintaining the appearance of fair treatment. Thus the principle of rewarding excellence serves to legitimize the unequal consequences of schooling by associating success with competence. At the same time, the institution of objectively administered tests of performance serves to allow a limited amount of upward mobility among exceptional children of the lower class, thus providing further legitimation of the operations of the social system by giving some credence to the myth of widespread mobility.

The second example is the principle that elementary and secondary schooling should be financed in very large measure schooling should be financed in very large measure from local revenues. This principle is supported on the grounds that it is necessary to preserve political liberty. Given the degree of residential segregation by income level, the effect of this principle is to produce an unequal distribution of school resources among children of different classes. Towns with a large tax base can spend large sums for the education of their disproportionately upper class children even without suffering a higher than average tax rate. Because the main resource inequalities in schooling thus exist between rather than within school districts, and because there is no effective mechanism for redistribution of school funds among school districts, poor families lack a viable political strategy for correcting the inequality.

The above rules of the game—rewarding "excellence" and financing schools locally—illustrate the complementarity between the political and economic power of the upper class. In each case, adherence to the rule has the effect of generating unequal consequences via a mechanism which operates largely outside the political system. As long as one adheres to the "reward excellence" principle, the responsibility for unequal results in schooling appears to lie outside the upper class, often in some fault of the poor—such as their class culture—which is viewed as lying beyond the reach of political action or criticism. Likewise, as long as the local financing of schools is maintained, the achievement of equality of resources among children of different social classes requires the class integration of school districts, an objective for which there are no effective political instruments as long as we allow a market in residential properties and an unequal distribution of income.

Thus it appears that the consequences of an unequal distribution of political power among classes complement the results of class culture in maintaining an educational system which has thus far been capable of transmitting status from generation to generation, and capable in addition of political survival in the formally democratic and egalitarian environment of the contemporary United States.

The role of the schools in reproducing and legitimizing the social division of labor has recently been challenged by popular egalitarian movements. At the same time, the educational system is showing signs of internal structural weakness. These two developments suggest that fundamental change in the schooling process may soon be possible. Analysis of both the potential and the limits of educational change will be facilitated by drawing together and extending the strands of the above argument.

4. The Limits Of Educational Reform

If the above attempt to identify the roots of inequality in U.S. education is convincing, it has done more than reconcile apparent discrepancies between the democratic forms and unequal content of U.S. education. For it is precisely the sources of educational inequality which we must understand in order to develop successful political strategies in the pursuit of educational equality.

I have argued that the structure of education reflects the social relations of production. For at least the past century and a half, expansion of education and changes in the forms of schooling have been responses to needs generated by the economic system. The sources of present inequality in U.S. education were found in the mutual reinforcement of class subcultures and social class biases in the operations of the school system itself. The analysis strongly suggests that educational inequalities are rooted in the basic institutions of our economy. Reconsideration of some of the basic mechanisms of educational inequality lends support to this proposition. First the principle of rewarding academic excellence in educational promotion and selection serves not only to legitimize the process by which the social division of labor is reproduced. It is also a basic part of the process which socializes young people to work for external rewards and encourages them to develop motivational structures fit for the alienating work of the capitalist economy. Selecting students form the bottom of the middle of the achievement scale for promotion to higher levels of schooling would go a long way towards equalizing education, but it would also jeopardize the schools' capacity to train productive and well-adjusted workers. Second, the way in which local financing of schools operates to maintain educational inequality is also rooted in the capitalist economy, in this case in the existence of an unequal distribution of income, free, markets in residential property, and the narrow limits of state, power. However, it seems unwise to emphasize this aspect of the long run problem of equality in education, for the inequalities in school resources resulting from the localization of finance may not be of crucial importance in maintaining inequalities in the effects of education. Moreover, it seems that a significant undermining of the principle of local finance may already be under way in response to pressures from the poorer states and school districts.

Of greater importance in the perpetuation of educational inequality are differential class subcultures. These class-based differences in personality, values, and expectations, I have argued, represent an adaptation to the different requirements of adequate work performance at various leaves in the hierarchical social relations of production. Class subcultures, then, stem from the everyday experiences of workers in the structure of production characteristic of capitalist societies.

It should be clear by this point that educational equality cannot be achieved through changes in the school system alone. Nonetheless, attempts at educational reform may move us closer to that objective if, in their failure, that lay bare the unequal nature of our school system and destroy the illusion of unimpeded mobility through education. Successful educational reforms reducing racial or class disparities in schooling, for example—may also serve the cause of equality of education for it seems likely that equalizing access to schooling will challenge the system either to make good its promise of rewarding educational attainment of find ways of coping with a mass disillusionment with the great panacea.

Yet if the record of the last century and a half of educational reforms is any guide, we should not expect radical change in education to result from the efforts of those confining their attention to the schools. The political victories of past reform movements have apparently resulted in little if any effective equalization. My interpretation of the educational consequences of class culture and class power suggests that these educational reform movements failed because they sought to eliminate equational inequalities without challenging the basic institutions of capitalism.

Efforts to equalize education through changes in government policy will at best scratch the surface of inequality. For much of the inequality in U.S. education has its origin outside the limited sphere of state power, in the hierarchy of work relations and the associated differences in class culture. As long as jobs are defined so that some have power over many and others have power over nothing—as long as the social division of labor persists—educational inequality will be built into U.S. society.

12

The School as a Mechanism of Social Differentiation

The standard approach to the study of students who are and are not admitted to college begins with examination of the characteristics of college-qualified graduates to determine how they differ from those of nonqualified students. The findings of investigations oriented by this approach suggest that the more "obvious" explanations, such as that the college-qualified students have higher I.Q. scores, higher grade records, greater financial support from their parents, etc., than their non-college-qualified peers, are inadequate to account for students who are qualified but do not get to college. For example, a recent volume reports a finding by Stouffer that many students with high I.Q. scores did not go to college. He reports also that of the high I.Q. students who did not go to college, many had consistently good academic records during their high school careers.

In view of such findings, social scientists have increasingly directed their attention to "non-intellective" determinants of educational, occupational, and general life aspirations. Among students whose tested capabilities and course grades are high, the determinants of college-going aspirations and actual college enrollment have been sought in cultural, social, and motivational factors. Performance and achievement are conceived to be products of ability and motivation when talent is above a minimum level considered necessary for success in college. Thus, Turner, using a sample of male college students, has investigated the motivational significance of the standards of reference groups used by future-oriented students to evaluate the relative success of their own performance. Strodtbeck has also emphasized the social and cultural motivational sources of academic achievement in his study of Jewish and Italian high school students. His findings suggest the motivational significance of group differences in family interaction, particularly power relations in the socialization process and value-orientations toward achievement. Similarly, Parsons, Kahl, and others have underlined the importance of social class membership as a major determinant of the occupational aspirations and achievement of youth. They have emphasized class-related differentials in the socialization of children and the consequences of such differences for the attitudes of youth toward academic achievement, occupational aspirations, and plans for college education.

Hollingshead's study of adolescence in Flmtown presents a somewhat different perspective on the relation between social class and the social as well as academic status of students within the school system. His concern with the organization of adolescent activities among the youth in Elmtown directed him to investigate the influences of social class membership upon clique formation and the effects of such cliques upon the treatment and evaluation of students by administrative and teaching personnel within the school. Since the publication of Hollings head's book, peer groups and related peer cultures and their influences upon the organization of adolescent attitudes, activities, and achievement have been subjects of sociological investigation, both theoretical and empirical. In his recent study, Coleman specifically examined these influences by investigating the normative effects of peer group climates upon the relative valuation of peer achievement in academic, athletic, and social activities among the student populations of ten high schools varying in size and organization.

In the following pages we present an alternative formulation that conceives of the differentiation of students as a consequence of the administrative organization and decisions of personnel in the high school. We shall contend that the distribution of students in such categories as college-qualified and non-college-qualified is to a large extent characteristic of the administrative organization of the high school and therefore can be explained in terms of that organization. We shall be concerned primarily with the relation between the administrative organization of the high school and the ways in which the students are processed through it. More specifically, we wish to investigate how the routine decisions of the guidance and counseling personnel within the high school are related to the college/non-college decisions and, by implication, to the occupational choices made by students.

Our more general concern with the allocation of personnel within the occupational structure of the larger society is similar to that of Parsons. We view as problematic, however, his assumption that the "virtually ascribed" college-going expectation among the middle and upper-class segments of the population *accounts for* the higher rate of students from those social classes who do in fact go to college. Although he identifies the school and prior academic achievement as the institutional setting within which the college-going expectation is expressed, he does not systematically consider how the formal organization of the school affects the realization of those expectations. In stressing the class ascribed character of the college aspiration, he assumes that the organizational processing of the aspiration if routine and non-problematic. We wish to question this assumption in our study.

Although heightened competition for college facilities has stimulated the growth and development of colleges throughout the nation, it has also given impetus to a policy of restricted enrollment for "quality" education and raised the entrance requirements among the "better" colleges to which students of the middle and upper social classes aspire. In view of the changing ratios of supply and demand in college facilities, it should also be noted that the theoretically significant distribution of high school seniors is not the gross college/non-college dichotomy, but the distribution of students according to their admission into colleges ranging from those having the highest applicant/enrollment ratio and admission requirements to those accepting any high school graduate. Class-ascribed college-going expectations might be considered an adequate explanation of the gross college/non-college distribution, but it cannot explain how students are distributed among hierarchically ranked (prestige) colleges. An explanation of such a distribution requires an investigation of the ways in which admission to various colleges is subject to specifically *organizational* contingencies.

Assuming that parents have college aspirations, to whatever quality of college, for their children, and assuming that their children have internalized those aspirations, whether or not such students do in fact become eligible for college entrance depends upon: (1) the communication by parents and/or the student to the school of the student's intention to prepare for college admission; (2) the enrollment of the student in high school courses that will qualify him for college—i.e., courses that will meet college entrance requirements; (3) the satisfactory completion such courses; and (4), in some....... of college/non-college or "good"/"better"/"best" college distributions of the student population, we do not deny that the formal organization of the high school progressively implements the college and occupational goals of the majority of students. Such student goals, however, are processed and actualized through a system subject to the contingencies of organizational processes. Indeed, it is precisely the routine aspects of the organizational processing activity that are of interest and are revealed by the variety of "problems" that attend the movement of a cohort of students through the high school system....

In order to obtain information concerning the process of student evaluation as practiced by the counseling personnel, we systematically questioned the counselor to whom the students in our sample were assigned. We were particularly interested in the criteria used in categorizing student achievement and in how the achievement-type classification compares with the "objective" measures of student ability (SCAT) and performance (grade-point average in the freshman year). The materials obtained in our interviews with this counselor are presented below.

The counselor's achievement types. When we asked the counselor how she would classify each of the students in our sample, she employed the following categories (which were widely used by the teaching as well as the counseling personnel at Lakeshore High) of classification: (1) "Excellent student," (2) "Average achiever." (3) "Underachiever," (4) "Overachiever," (5) "Opportunity student." Asked what she considered the most stable basis for her judgment of a student, she replied:

"Probably ability —that's the most specific and measurable."

Table 1. Counselor's Achievement Types by SCAT Scores and Ninth-grade Point Average

Achievement types	*Ninth-grade point average* 1.00-1.50	1.75-2.00	2.25-3.00	3.25-4.00	4.25-5.00	*N*
Opportunity				(06)(10)	(01)(02)	9
student			(15)	(12)(16)	(02)(13)	
Overachiever		(42)	(27)	(16)		3
Underachiever			(68)(68)	(17)(39)	(10)(39)	
		(68)	(73)(80)(84)	(58)(75)(78)		18
			(87)(90)(96)	(80)(93)		
Average		(47)(64)	(27)(32)(35)	(15)(20)(20)	(28)	
achiever		(64)(75)	(39)(50)(64)	(35)(42)(42)	(39)	33
			(64)(68)(68)	(50)(52)(54)		
			(68)(68)(73)	(75)		
			(73)(78)(84)			
			(87)(90)			
Excellent	(73)(73)(80)	(75)(78)				
student	(84)(85)(94)	(84)(84)	(94)	(90)		18
	(95)(97)	(90)(93)				
		(95)(96)				
N	8	14	28	23	9	81*

*No information for 8 cases.

Interviewer: "And how do you determine ability?"

Counselor: "By tests and performance, generally."

If we assume that the counselor's evaluation of student performance is to assess the students' progress in the courses to which they have been assigned, we would expect a systematic relationship between the achievement-type classification and the distribution of SCAT/grade-point discrepancies. In Table 1 we have included the SCAT scores and grade-point averages of each of the students classified by the counselor in order to show the relation between discrepancies and achievement types. An examination of the table will show the range of discrepancies classified in the five achievement types by the counselor. (The range of discrepancies for each category of achievement types is summarized in Table 2.) For example, the "excellent student" category includes 9 students with SCAT scores of 90-95 and with grade-point averages ranging from 1.00 to 3.25. On the other hand, the 2.25-3.00 grade-point column shows that there are 4 students with SCAT scores of 90-95, but 2 are classified as "underachievers," another as an "average achiever," and the fourth as an "excellent student." These classifications are not a strict application of the SCAT/grade point discrepancy criterion. The classification of other students (e.g., the SCAT 68/1.75-2.00 "underachiever," the SCAT 17/3.25-4.00 "underachiever," the SCAT 47/1.75-2.00 "average achiever," etc.) provides added evidence that the criterion is not consistently applied and does not account for the distribution of achievement

Table 2. Range of SCAT and Ninth-grade Point Average by Counselor's Classification of Achievement Types

Achievement types	*SCAT range*	*Grade-point range*	*N*
Excellent student	73-97	1.00-3.25	18
Average achiever	15-90	1.75-4.25	33
Underachiever	10-96	2.00-4.66	18
Overachiever	16-42	2.00-3.75	3
Opportunity student	01-16	3.00-5.00	9
			81*

*No information for 8 cases.

types. The table shows that neither SCAT nor grade point alone accounts for the achievement-type classifications.

The inconsistencies revealed in this classification of students are of more than passing interest, for the achievement types are not merely descriptive categories to the personnel who use them. The classification of students as achievement types in effect produces a distribution of students who are conceived by the organizational personnel to have "problems." With the exception of students classified, by whatever criteria, as "average achiever" and "excellent student," the achievement-type classification identifies those students who are performing below the level of their ability ("underachiever") or above it ("overachiever"), or who are lacking in both ability and performance ("opportunity student"). In the following chapter we shall discuss how these "problems" are articulated with the organizational activities of counselors at Lakeshore High and 19 other high schools. We wish here to pursue further the criteria applied in the process of evaluating student performance.

If the more or less "rational criterion" of SCAT/grade-point discrepancy does not account for the counselor's achievement-type classification of students, what are the bases of her judgments? What are the variables that might operate to produce the variations in the distribution discussed above? Social-class characteristics of the student population, commonly found by social researchers to influence the evaluations of students by school personnel, are variables that deserve examination. In our investigation of this possibility we were directed by our theoretical orientation, which emphasizes the vocabulary and syntax used by the organizational personnel, to obtain the social-class categories that *the counselor* used to differentiate the student population.

The counselor's social types. To explore the relation between the stratification system as perceived by the counselor and her classification of achievement types, we questioned her as follows:

a: How many social statuses, that is, social-class groups,

would you say there are here at Lakeshore High School?

b: How would you describe, in general, each of the groups you mentioned?

c: How would you place each of the students named on these cards (handling her a set of cards with the names of all the students in our sample) into each of the groups you mentioned?

The phrasing of the questions assumes that social-status categories are recognized, if not employed, by the counselor as one dimension of her classification of students. The questions, however, allow the counselor to interpret "social status, that is, social-class groups" in her own terms. We would expect the counselor to base her evaluations on the same kind of common-sense criteria one would expect from persons in the general population—i.e., the categories and criteria should be characteristically general, vaguely defined, and perhaps inconsistently applied.

When the counselor was asked question *a*, she offered without prompting from the interviewer a description of each group as she identified them. That is, the interviewer found it unnecessary to ask question *b*. The counselor's categories and comments were as follows:

1. First there's the main group—the in-group. This is the group that belongs to the "Y." They head this group, they're at the forefront of the activities in the school, they're the leaders. Most of them live in Lakeshore. They belong to the Presbyterian Church there, or is it a Methodist Church?
2. Then there's the group just below this group. They're trying the attain the [main] group. They're sometimes included in the activities of the first group, but they don't really belong. They might be the campaign managers for members of the first group if they're running for an office. This group will do almost anything to get into the other group.
3. There's the other element. These students would not at

all consider getting into the first group. They get into a lot of trouble, they have difficulties with their studies. Most of the drop outs are from this group—they drop out at 16 or 17.

4. We can't deny that there's a Negro group here at Lakeshore. They have their own group, their own identification. In some instances there are those who cut across the line, but they don't participate in their "Y" activities. The "Y" seems to be the center of activities, and the "Y" is a segregated group.

5. Then there's the group that's left [not politically left, but left by subtraction]. This is not really a group. They don't have a group of their own. There are some strong individualists in this group.

6. We should make some note of these other students who are not in a group. They are noteworthy individuals. Because they are outstanding they are known to everybody. But they don't belong to any group. They're the kind that might wear black leotards or carry a guitar. They're a group, but not a group. They come to our attention in some way they're outstanding scholastically, or they're extremely sensitive, [the counselor smiled here, which was interpreted to mean that she did not want to be more explicit] or intelligent. Some of them are referred for psychiatric care. [The counselor cited the case of a student in our sample who would fit this group. She called this group "loners."]

7. [The counselor then mentioned another group who were "like loners" but she said they were "rebelling." This group dressed, she said, in extreme fashion.] They wear their skirts too short. [In our sample, this group consists of four or five girls who are described as being tightly banded together, but who are not though to have the "nerve" to do anything as individuals.] They find it difficult to fit into things at Lakeshore High. Anything

typical of teenage here is ridiculous for them. [The counselor stated that the "loner" described in the last group might wear leotards or braids or carry a guitar even if no one else were doing so.]

The counselor's response to question *a* indicates that the interpreted "social status, that is, social class" to mean different *social types* of students within the stratification system of the high school, and we shall refer to them hereafter by that term. With the exception of Social Types 1 and 2, and perhaps the "Negro group" (Social Type 4), her descriptions do not necessarily imply a strict hierarchical ranking in the conventional terms of social class. The pluralistic classification appears to be based on some combination of aspiration, rejection, or withdrawal of students from participation in school and out-of-school social activities.

Table 3. Counselor's Social Types by Counselor's Classification of Achievement Designations

	Achievement types					
Social types	*Excel.*	*Aver.*	*Under*	*Over*	*Oppor.*	*N*
7	0	1	0	1	1	3
6	1	0	0	0	0	1
5	0	10	7	1	4	22
4	0	1	0	0	2	3
30	0	2	4	0	1	7
2	4	16	6	1	2	29
1	12	2	1	0	0	15
N	17	32	18	3	10	80*

*No information on 9 cases.

In response to question *c*, the counselor classified the students in our sample into the categories that she enumerated and described. Table 3 shows the relation between her social-type and achievement-type classifications of students. Twelve of the 17 students classified as "excellent students" were also classified as Social

Type 1. Conversely, all but 3 of the 15 social Type 1 students were classified as "excellent students." In none of the remaining categories in which the frequencies are large enough to warrant consideration (i.e., Social Types 2 and 5, and the achievement types of "average achiever" and "underachiever") is there a suggested relationship which approaches that between the "excellent student" Social Type 1 classification.

It would appear that there is a fusion of academic and social-type criteria in the counselor's classification of the "excellent" social Type 1 student. Table 4, which presents the distribution of social types with reference to the students' SCAT scores and grade-point averages, provides a clue to the nature of the academic criteria that may have been applied by the counselor in the social-type classification. With one exception (one student with SCAT of 68), all students in Social Type 1 have SCAT scores of 73 or higher, but their grade-point averages range from 1.00 to 4.00. The classification of the 94/2.25-3.00 student and the 90/3.25-4.00 student in Social Type 1 shows that these relatively large SCAT/grade-point discrepancies (indicating underachievement) did not disqualify them from inclusion in this category. We note, however, that although high SCAT appears to be a characteristic of Social Type 1 students, there is an equal number of students with scores of 73 or higher who were classified in other social type categories.

The characterization of the "excellent" Social Type 1 student that may be made from Tables 3 and 4 is that of a student whom the counselor considers to be a "leader," who is in the "main group," and who has a relatively high SCAT score even if he does not have a high grade-point average.

Table 4 also indicates that neither SCAT nor grade-point average separately nor the discrepancy between them is systematically related to the classification of social types. Our materials suggest that the counselor's social-type classification does not account for the majority of her achievement-type classification of students.

Table 4. Counselor's Social Types by SCAT Scores and Ninth-grade Point Average

	Ninth-grade point average					
Social type	*1.00-1.50*	*1.75-2.00*	*2.25-3.00*	*3.25-4.00*	*4.25-5.00*	*N*
7				(15)	(13)	2
6	(97)					1
5		(47)	(15)(27) (32)(39)(64) (68)(68)(73) (80)	(17)(20) (35)(52) (58)	(02)(07) (10)	18
4			(78)	(06)(50) (10)(12)	(01)	4
3				(39)(42) (54)(78)	(39)	7
2	(85)	(42)(64) (64)(75) (90)(93)	(27)(35)(50) (64)(68)968) (84)(84)(87) (87)(90)(90) (96)	(16)(20) (42)(75) (93)	(02)	26
1	(73)(73) (80)(84) (94)(95)	(68)(75) (78)(84) (84)(95) (96)	(73)(73) (94)	(75)(90)		18
N	8	14	27	21	7	76*

*No information for 13 cases.

The counselor's social-class ratings. The counselor's response to question a raised the question of whether or not she differentiated students by social-class categories in the conventional sense. If so, would her classification of students in those terms better account for the achievement types than the social types? To obtain this information, we explained to the counselor that we would like her to classify our student sample into five strata of social classes. Using a fivefold classification, we presented these strata to her as: Class 1, Upper;

Class II, Lower Upper; Class III, Upper Middle; Class IV, Lower Middle; and Class V, Lower. No further criteria for the classification of students, except as indicated immediately below, were given to the counselor. When she was presented with these strata, the counselor asked:

What do you mean by "upper"? In Lakeshore that would have to be old-guard Lakeshore. There may be some with more money but they wouldn't be old guard. For example, the — Boy's family has lots of money, but they don't make it on the old guard.

Interviewer: So, the — boy would not be placed in the "upper class if that's true:

Table 5 shows the social-class distribution that resulted from the counselor's classification of students by achievement-type categories. It would be noted that although the counselor indicated by her remark about the "old-guard Lakeshore" that she recognized the existence of an "upper" class, she did not assign any of the students in our sample to that social class. As in the case of Social Type 1, "excellent students" are predominantly from one category-all but one in Social Class II. The converse relationship, however, does not obtain: i.e., only 40 per cent (17 out of 42) Class

Table 5. Distribution of Achievement Types by Counselor's Social-class Ratings

	Counselor's social class ratings					
Achievement *types*	*I*	*II*	*III*	*IV*	*V*	*N*
Opportunity		2	1	4	2	9
Overachiever		2	1			3
Underachiever		10	5	4		19
Average achiever		12	13	5	1	31
Excellent		17	1			18
N		42	21	13	3	80*

*No information on 9 cases.

II students are classified as "excellent students." Thus, although the social-class category adds the characteristic of social Class II to the description of the "excellent student," it does no better than the social-type classification in suggesting the basis for the over-all distribution of achievement types....

Individual Effort and Organizational Sponsorship

Our study provides illustrative data that are relevant for an examination of Turner's analysis of the two educational systems. His analysis proceeds on the assumption that

> ...within a formally open class system that provides for mass education the organizing folk norm which defines the accepted mode of upward mobility is a crucial factor in shaping the school system, and may be even more crucial than the extent of upward mobility.

He proposes that the organizing folk norm in the United States differs from that in England and as a consequence the relation of the two systems of education to the processes of social mobility are characteristically different. The American and British educational systems are characterized in the following ideal typical terms: *Contest* mobility is a system in which elite status is the prize in an open contest and is taken by the aspirants' own efforts. While the "contest" is governed by some rules of fair play, the contestants have wide latitude in the strategies they may employ. Since the "prize" of successful upward mobility is not in the hands of an established elite to give out the latter can not determine who shall attain it and who shall not. Under *sponsored* mobility elite recruits are chosen by the established elite or their agents, and elite status is *given* on the basis of some criterion of supposed merit and cannot be *taken* by any amount of effort or strategy. Upward mobility is like entry into a private club where each candidate must be "sponsored" by one or more of the members. Ultimately the members grant or deny upward mobility on the basis of whether they judge the candidate to have those qualities they wish to see in fellow members.

Turner's characterization of the American educational system as one that promotes a contest among individuals who "have wide latitude in the strategies they may employ" to facilitate their mobility must be modified if our illustrative materials are indicative of a trend in American high schools. Our materials indicate first of all that in the bureaucratically organized high school the day-to-day activities of the school personnel effectively control the access of students to the limited number of curriculums available, particularly their access to the curriculum most instrumental for upward mobility, i.e., the college preparatory curriculum. Our case study suggests that through their control over the student's course programs, the school personnel may include or exclude students from the "contest" and that the "aspirants' own efforts" are neither the only nor the critical determinant of their qualification as "contestants."

This is not to say that the aspirants' efforts are irrelevant to qualifying them for the "contest" or advancing their position within it, but rather that their efforts are not necessarily evaluated, as might be assumed, by academic standards alone. If the SCAT scores and grade-point averages of students may be considered indicative of their efforts, our materials suggest that, in a number of cases, students who show such effort may be handicapped or even excluded from the "contest."

It should be noted that the educational system in the United States does manifest all the formal characteristics that Turner attributes to contest mobility. There is an emphasis upon periodic examinations; formalized criteria govern the progress of students in the hierarchy of grade levels; college entrance requirements are not automatically achieved by virtue of enrollment in high school; and college admission is an outcome of a competitive process. Our research, however, supports the view that the student's progress in this sequence of transitions is contingent upon the interpretations, judgments, and action of school personnel vis-a-vis the student's biography, social and personal "adjustment," appearance and demeanor, social class, and "social type" as well as his demonstrated ability and performance. In this respect, mobility in the highly bureaucratized high school bears a striking resemblance to the sponsorship found in graduate departments of universities, in which judgments about the student's maturity, emotional stability, character, and personal appearance are often important determinants of his social mobility.

Secondly, although Turner assumes that the folk norm of contest mobility is "present at least implicitly in people's thinking, guiding their judgements of what is appropriate in many specific matters," the degree to which such thinking is articulated in the organizational judgments and actions of the school personnel must be viewed as problematic. This is particularly true in an educational system in which school policies are increasingly professionalized and bureaucratically implemented. The advances and setbacks in the process of mobility in such a system are governed less by the folk norms of the larger society than by the doctrines and practices of a professionalized bureaucracy. Insofar as the rationalization and bureaucratization of procedures imply greater "objectivity" in the evaluation of performance and distribution of rewards, it might be argued that the application of such organizational techniques represents an institutionalization of the folk norm of contest mobility. Our materials do not support such an argument. Examination of how students are assigned to college and non-college curriculums, distributed among different ability-grouped courses, and identified as various "problems" suggests that the professed ideal of equal access to educational opportunities for those of equal ability is not necessarily served by such procedures.

Indeed, our materials on the differential interpretation of test scores and grade-point averages by school personnel, the definitions and treatment of student "problems," and the organizational activities directed toward facilitating the processing of low performance students toward college entrance indicate that the patterned deviations from bureaucratic procedures amounts to a form of sponsorship. The differentiation of students by objective criteria obviously is not the rational basis for the allocation of educational opportunities, for the bureaucracy permits considerable discretion in decision-making. The views of professional educators concerning.

"adjustment," "motivation," "realistic goals," "overachievers," "participation," and the like are accommodated in the bureaucratic setting, and they constitute significant qualifications of the folk norm of contest mobility. The accommodation of such conceptions has created a complicated system of organizational sponsorship in which discrepancies of ability and performance, aspirations, and realistic possibilities are adjusted, modified, or created in some instances, ignored in others. Decisions for such actions are made, by professionals who are guided not by folk norms but by explicit and implicit educational doctrines and practices.

The organizational sponsorship that occurs in American schools may not be as obvious or as explicitly acknowledged as the form of sponsorship that Turner attributes to the British schools. It is quite clear that even in Hollingshead's class-conscious Elmtown the differential treatment and sponsorship of students by school personnel were covertly practiced. Although the bureaucratic organization of the modern comprehensive high school is undoubtedly less vulnerable to the inequities of the socialclass pressures documented by Hollingshead, the distribution of educational opportunities is conditioned by decisions and actions that effectively accommodate social-class as well as other information about students.

The rationalization of the school system through the incorporation of the concepts and methods of psychiatry, psychology, and the social sciences has legitimized the relevance of personal and social factors for the interpretation of the "objective" measures of the student's ability and performance. Such factors are explicitly acknowledged as educationally relevant and incorporated into a complex system of organizational policies and procedures. Thus, although testing procedures are extensively employed and course grades are routinely reviewed, the information they provide are in some instances the sole basis for organizational decisions, but in other instances their significance is qualified by considerations of personal and social factors. In such a system, a student's mobility may be more than incidentally contingent upon the sponsorship of organizational personnel who certify him to be a "serious, personable, well-rounded student with leadership potential."

In presenting these objections to Turner's thesis we stress once again the importance of investigating the processes of social mobility at the level of the day-to-day organizational activities in which often unstated rules of mobility are defined and the direction and rate of progress through the system are controlled.

13

Turning Schools into Learning Institutions

That school administrators should regularly evaluate the achievements of school programs seems obvious. Yet schools have seldom made any serious effort to assess the performance of either existing programs or major innovations. This failure poses fundamental problems for performance improvement in general. How can schools hope to improve systematically without ascertaining what is and is not currently working?

Innovative programs for schools come from a variety of sources: education schools, policy institutes, textbook publishers, teachers' unions, individual district program offices, and teachers and principals themselves. Individual schools and school districts may adopt these programs for may reasons, from resolving a crisis to improving an already successful organizational structure, and they may adapt the program to fit the particular local circumstances. Once they have put programs in place, few schools make any serious effort to gather information about how well they are working—unless they are obviously broken.

Two reasons underlie this reluctance to judge. The first is that defining success in schooling is hard. Intuitively, school personnel have long resisted standardized testing and assessment. Instead of using a fixed set of criteria to evaluate students, educators have preferred more flexible systems that allow each student to emphasize his or her own achievements. Yet flexible measurement quickly degenerates into a collection of semi-independent observations and impressions that cannot be compared. The second difficulty in assessing schools is establishing responsibility and developing appropriate accountability. Even if some measurement of performance is accepted, using it to assign praise or blame is difficult because so little is understood of the inner workings of the education process. Schools, as we have repeatedly stressed, are just one part of education, and schools themselves are complicated institutions involving many components.

Evaluating the past effectiveness of school programs is difficult enough, but the reforms we propose add new challenges for evaluation. The performance incentives proposed in the last chapter would move schools into uncharted waters. Instituting such reforms would demand a commitment to evaluation unlike any that has ever before existed in education. Moreover, if progress is to occur at an acceptable pace and with an acceptable amount of uncertainty, new approaches to developing information will be necessary.

At a minimum, successful evaluation will require new leadership from state and federal government to help create measurement techniques, to develop ongoing evaluations, and to disseminate accurate information. In describing the new roles of governments in the last chapter, we underscored the need for experimentation with alternative incentive schemes. A well-designed program of experimentation and systematic evaluation of the components of incentive schemes will lead to more rapid accumulation of knowledge. But, beyond that, explicit attention to random assignment experimentation, described below, offers even greater possibilities for learning. These evaluation approaches nonetheless require significant changes in the way the business of education is conducted.

Some argue that improved student testing and assessment can lead reform by itself. With accurate assessments of student performance from tests, runs the argument, schools will automatically focus on improving test scores: teachers will adjust to improve student achievement, management decisions will become obvious, and reform will occur almost spontaneously. We know of no evidence to suggest this is a realistic expectation. We wholeheartedly support the development of higher standards and improved measures of performance. But we doubt that they will be good enough in a variety of relevant dimensions to carry reform.

Two parallel developments are necessary to improve the ability of educators to evaluate the school system. A systematic approach to experimentation and evaluation of school programs must be developed and instituted, and the assessment of student achievement must be refined and improved. These two facets of improving the knowledge base are obviously interrelated, but they can be most clearly understood if discussed separately.

Finally, it must be underscored that virtually no progress will occur without regular measurement of success and failure. Indeed, a primary reason for believing that school reform is necessary is that available measures of student performance trace the problems. Although some would minimize or discard evidence from editing standardized tests, perhaps arguing that conceptually superior measures should be used, it would be a mistake to do so without an operationally useful alternative. Existing measures of performance, although flawed in some ways, still can provide useful information about the success of schools, programs, and approaches. The suggestions that follow below about various improvements, particularly for direct use in incentive plans, should not be interpreted as a wholesale condemnation of existing tests for evaluative purposes. Instead these proposals outline a plan of development and improvement.

The Varied Uses of Performance Assessments

Historically, schools have concentrated their assessment efforts on the progress and performance of individual students. Course grades, written comments on student development, and, more recently, performance on standardized tests all provide information on how well each student is doing. These assessments are based both on absolute standards, such as whether the student meets certain specified learning goals, and on relative standards, such as how the student compares with peers in the classroom and across the country. These assessments give teachers information they can use to develop educational strategies for both groups and individuals.

Individual assessments also create incentives that motivate students to study. A key factor in the strength of those incentives, however, is the degree to which assessment information is made public and used to judge the student. Promotion through the grades, graduation, and the like constitute an important part of the public's general knowledge about individual students, providing strong incentives for them to perform well in those terms. Scores on standardized tests and course grades are sometimes used to make judgments about students, for example in the college application process, but frequently they are not made generally public, thus lessening the incentives for students to perform well. Employers virtually never review student transcripts, so course grades consequently hold less importance for many students.

Assessments of student performance have uses in addition to shaping students' careers. Most obviously, they can and should be a part of both new and existing efforts to evaluate the programs teaching those students. Reforms designed to introduce performance incentives heighten the importance of program evaluation and student assessment. If rewards are linked to student performance, teachers, principals, and other school personnel can more clearly focus their efforts on the prime task of education. But such linkage requires accurate and consistent evaluation of performance, which is relatively uncomplicated and inexpensive to provide. It also requires assessment techniques that are subtly, but importantly, different from those used to measure students. Comparing the performance of a student to the other members of the same class is one thing. Comparing the performance of that class, as a group, to peers across the nation is harder. And assessing the contribution made by individual teachers and administrators to that performance is harder still. Yet all three types of assessments must be done if reform is to drive forward.

Key Ingredients of Performance Measurement for Management

The ultimate point of evaluating education is to improve the management and operations of schools by providing both a grounding for policy decisions and incentives for teachers, students, and other school personnel to perform well. As such, assessments will inevitably be controversial, for they not only effect the careers of those in the schools, but they also implicitly define the objectives of the school system.

A good assessment must be linked to the objectives of the educational system. As with many aspects of education, though, this apparently simple requirement is much easier to state than to implement. Many school goals are imprecisely defined, and, therefore, are not very helpful in designing measurement systems. Many educators who try to make the goals more specific tend to be overly inclusive; school objectives come to touch upon every conceivable aspect of life and learning and are thus cumbersome to use in the day-do-day management of schools. Pennsylvania's attempt to adopt an outcome-based education system, for example, illustrates many of the problems of achieving consensus on manageable goals for schools (box 13-1).

There are two natural starting points for creating educational goals and developing techniques to measure progress toward them. One, now most commonly used, is to build upon the objectives of the school curriculum. When states define school programs, most stipulate the courses the students must complete and the material those sources must cover. Implicitly, these objectives define what a student must achieve to move on to the next grade. These goals form an obvious starting place for assessment.

A second, often neglected, starting point for setting educational goals is career skills. For most students and their parents the raisin d'être of schools is preparation for useful and rewarding careers. So the acquisition of job skills is an obvious candidate to be represented in performance assessment. Job skills, however, should not be viewed simply as those taught in the traditional vocational

Box13-1. Outcome-Based Education in Pennsylvania

In 1990 Pennsylvania's state board of education began a review of its regulations on curricula, instruction, and assessment. Frustrated with the results of earlier attempts at school reform, the board proposed the idea of outcome-based education, following an emerging national trend favoring the evaluation of schools based on the performance of students, as opposed to school inputs (such as course work).

After countless hearings and meetings, the state board of education in March 1992 voted to make Pennsylvania the first state in the nation to adopt a statewide policy of outcome-based education. Months of protests and delays ensued. The board eventually approved a list of fifty-five educational outcomes in January 1993. Instead of following a fixed curriculum, students would be required to meet each of these outcomes to graduate from high school. Only one month after the agenda was approved, however, Pennsylvania's House of Representatives voted overwhelmingly to nullify the outcome-based regulations. Finally, in summer 1993 a new, reduced set of objectives became the governing objective for Pennsylvania schools.

Proponents of Pennsylvania's outcome-based education believe that eliminating input regulations will improve schools by allowing them to focus on student achievement. By giving teachers and administrators flexibility in devising curricula and instruction, reformers hope to encourage the creation of innovative strategies to meet the high standards set for students and to use resources more efficiently. Finally, they argue that focusing on outcomes provides greater accountability.

Conversely, opponents of outcome-based education believe that the reform is too drastic a change to be undertaken without any valid research to support it. They believe that some of the board's outcomes focus on student attitudes and values rather than on cognitive ability and that it is not the state's business to meddle in those areas. Moreover, even the academic outcomes are defined very vaguely, giving teachers, textbook writers, and test developers little guidance. Opponents further argue that assessment systems, newly developed to measure student performance, are too subjective and expensive and that provisions for remedial education are insufficient. Because outcome-based education eliminates course work requirements that ensure that schools offer certain subjects, opponents fear that some schools will reduce their curricula. Moreover, outcome-based education could require less effort of top students. The net effect, say the opponents, will be to lower educational performance rather than to raise it.

Pennsylvania's experience amply demonstrates the potential problems that arise when schools shift to outcome standards. To begin with, the program has not been completely developed and has not been demonstrated to be reliable enough to drive the entire system. The incentives for good performance and the sanctions for bad performance are largely undefined, making the efficacy of the system uncertain. Finally, the system is based heavily on the development of strategic plans by districts and on the certification of these plans by the state board of education, but there is no evidence that either group has sufficient capacity to do these well. Thus, although the sentiment behind the state's outcome-based education policy is consistent with the recommendations of this report, the state may have created insurmountable problems by introducing the system without first having done some experimentation and evaluation.

Sources: Rothman (1993); Harp (1993); Diegmueller (1993b); Pennsylvania State Board of Education (1993); Ravitch (1994).

education courses. Indeed, the evidence suggests that the career skills most highly demanded in the labor market are general communication and analytical skills, logical reasoning ability, and the like. These are general skills that till students should be taught and that should also represent the core of assessment systems. In addition, schools can and do improve parenting skills, make citizens more informed voters, discourage crime, and the like. Such external goals may also play a part in assessment and evaluation, although care need be taken when extending goals beyond academic and career kills to avoid creating measurement systems that are unworkably diffuse.

In addition to focusing on the objectives of schooling, a good assessment plan must be consistent and precise. To be useful in managing schools and providing incentives for school personnel, assessment schemes must separate the effects of schools from other factors that also influence student performance. Teachers can be confronted with students who are unprepared for any number of reasons: inadequate previous schooling, lack of motivation, little help from parents, or physical or mental limitations. Teachers may perform their own jobs better if they are aware of these other factors, but teachers should not be evaluated on factors over which they have no control. Similarly, allowance should be made for schools that receive ill-prepared students. In other words, the evaluation must allow assessment of value added by the school and teacher, that is, assessment of precisely what the schools contribute to the student's learning. Too often evaluators look only at absolute performance levels, instead of the value added.

Central-city schools, for example, are frequently condemned as failures without considering the overwhelming problems they face. Even the best teacher may not be able to transform an innercity seventh grader reading at the fourth-grade level into an eighth grader reading at the eighth-grade level. Nonetheless, a teacher who could bring that student up to the sixth-grade level by the end of the year would be doing a spectacular job, even though the improvement would not be sufficient to overcome the initial deficit. Just the opposite occurs in many affluent suburban districts, where the high level of achievement the student initially brings to class may mask poor teacher performance. The schools in these areas willingly take credit for the high absolute level of their students, even though their value added might be low.

High overall performance must be the final goal, but the best way to achieve that goal is to evaluate and reward programs, teachers, and schools according to what they contribute to individual student performance. Measures of total levels of performance will inevitably include influences outside of the school's control.

Forms of Testing and Measurement

Much of the current controversy about performance measurement in the schools revolves around student testing. Tests are alternately seen as a useless administrative burden, as a comprehensive force for low standards and mediocrity of schooling, or as America's best hope for driving performance improvements through reluctant school administrations. All of these views have some validity. Done well, however, testing has a crucial role to play in the process of learning about education that is the heart of school reform. The challenge is to ensure that testing is done well.

Standardized Testing

In recent years standardized tests have assumed an ever larger role in evaluating student performance. Many states now require periodic examinations using standardized tests. Data on average performance on those tests, broken down by district and often by individual schools, are frequently made available to the public. The availability of such information and the attention paid to it in the media and elsewhere has led to intense debate about the usefulness and appropriateness of standardized tests as a measure of school performance.

Properly done, standardized testing offers a level of objectivity and comparability that is unavailable from other sources. By applying a universal yardstick of student achievement, such tests have obvious advantages over other, subjective evaluations of performance. Tests can be used to evaluate differences in achievement among groups of students, say, in several schools with different programs. They can also indicate patterns of change in achievement levels.

The use of standardized tests, however, can also lead to unreliable conclusions about student performance. Many different tests are available, and the question "what to measure?" is one of the most contentious issues in standardized testing. To know what skills to measure, schools must first decide what skills they are seeking to produce. For example, a well-constructed test of Urdu might indicate which students knew that language, but, without a consensus that all students should learn Urdu, the test provides neither an overall assessment of educational achievement nor the basis for a comparison of achievement among schools. Consensus on the overall goals of American education has, at least in the past, been elusive. The future may be better, however, as efforts to develop national goals and standards begin to pay off.

Widespread testing entails hazards as well as difficulties. High-stakes testing, such as that required for high school graduation, where the results are perceived to have strong effects on students or school personnel, can lead to several unproductive outcomes. Teachers may emphasize material expected to be on the tests to the exclusion of all other material. Schools may overtly distort the results by selecting only certain students to take the tests.

Some schools are even rumored to have misreported results of student examinations.

The final, and most common, complaint about standardized testing is that many available testing systems do not accurately measure the range of material and skills that should be taught in schools. By overemphasizing testing, teachers and administrators neglect more complicated or creative tasks, which are not easy to test but which are still important to their students' education. Research on the accuracy of standardized tests is ambiguous, but addressing concerns of inaccuracy should form a key part of a program designed to use standardized tests more effectively. Such a program should consist of four parts.

First, research should be devoted to defining more clearly just what skills and achievements standardized tests should attempt to measure. This effort should be broadly based and solicit advice of people outside the standard schooling and testing groups, such as businesses. Second, because the range of items that can be tested effectively is limited, standardized tests cannot be the sole measure of performance. Other measures need be designed to complement standardized tests, particularly when the tests are components of a reward system. Third, because existing tests are subject to misuse and can bias instruction in undesirable ways, extreme caution must be exercised in rewarding teachers and school personnel for high test scores. Although results of standardized tests might form part of the evaluation of teachers, exclusive reliance on test results is likely to damage the quality of teaching. Downplaying the importance of scores is not particularly limiting to teacher evaluations, however, because principals are able to identify good performance without relying on test results. Fourth, test performance for individual students must be traced over time so that growth in achievement, instead of the absolute level of achievement, becomes the object of attention.

Although many have looked to testing to play a crucial role in driving reform, today's standardized tests cannot fulfill the reformers' high expectations. Current testing is not sufficiently accurate to pinpoint differences in the achievement of individual schools. More important, differences in school curricula make standardized measures hard to devise. Broad tests, of the kind that can encompass the inevitable differences in goals and emphasis from school to school, do not provide accurate and detailed data about differences among teachers and their classroom performance. Particularly in the near term, at the level of the school and classroom, more direct evaluation by the principal (and perhaps teachers and other personnel) is likely to provide more accurate information.

At the same time, standardized tests remain one of the best instruments for programmatic evaluation available today. Standardized tests can provide objective comparisons of basic skill development that facilitate hard decisionmaking about what is and is not working. These tests can be improved, but their usefulness for evaluative purposes is undeniable.

Authentic Tests

To overcome the difficulties of standardized tests, several educators have recently embarked on new and diverse approaches that promise richer views of student performance. Whether it is called "authentic testing," "genuine testing," or "performance-based testing," this approach is based on the notion that open-ended responses to standardized tasks and questions will allow better assessment of a student's true performance levels. Short answers, essays, math problems without multiple-choice answers, and more creative activities, such as writing poetry or personal narratives, form the basis for such assessments.

In addition to painting a better picture of an individual students' abilities and skills, authentic testing can also more effectively measure the broad range of analytical tasks that schools should be developing. Indeed, the time-honored tradition of individual evaluation within the classroom uses a similar approach. Such testing permits the teacher to make more precise assessments of the strengths and weaknesses of individual students.

Experience with authentic tests is limited, and work on many facets of such tests is in its infancy. Therefore, much of the current discussion is based on speculation and extrapolation of what might be developed. Clearly, authentic testing will always be more expensive and time-consuming to administer and evaluate than standardized tests based on multiple-choice responses. Thus, any potential gains will have to be compared with the added costs. The General Accounting Office has estimated that authentic tests might typically cost about twice as much as multiple-choice tests. The higher cost can be easily justified, however, if it results in more accurate measurements of student performance and in improved school efficiency.

Larger concerns about authentic testing center on the comparability of scores, both among groups of students and over time. Because the scoring of most authentic tests is subjective, many question the reliability of any resulting quantitative summary. Some uses of testing do not require explicit quantitative scores, however. For example, individual teachers do not necessarily require such information. Reliability is an important issue when performance measures are used to compare students in different schooling situations as part of an assessment of the effectiveness of schools, for example. Vermont's full-scale use of portfolio testing, a specialized form of authentic testing, provides mixed evidence about the reliability of such devices, although an entire testing project has not yet been completely developed (box 13-2). The same issues and questions arise over using authentic tests to measure the value added of teachers and schools to the progress of individual students.

The (often offsetting) advantages and disadvantages of standardized and authentic testing suggest that schools should consider using a combination of both. The choice of which to use in any specific situation depends on the kind of information needed. For detailed assessment of student performance, authentic testing offers clear advantages in the depth and richness of data. For overall assessments of the educational system involving direct comparisons of performance, standardized, multiple-choice tests may offer equally clear advantages, particularly when measuring basic skills

Box 13-2. Vermont Portfolio Scores

Vermont introduced an innovative assessment system in 1988, when it began exploring the use of portfolios of a student's best work in mathematics and writing. That system is now employed statewide in grades four and eight. Although the program has been in effect for a limited period, early evaluations of its successes and failures provide useful insights into the use of portfolios and other types of authentic tests.

Because it previously had no statewide assessment system, Vermont wanted to use its new program both to provide information on student performance and to encourage improved teaching. In mathematics teachers construct portfolios of five to seven pieces of the student's best work covering puzzle solving, applications, and investigations. In writing teachers choose six to eight different pieces, such as poems, short stories, and personal narrations. Each portfolio is submitted for scoring by other teachers. There are also objective examinations of certain content areas, although these are not necessarily multiple-choice examinations.

The Rand Cooperation evaluated Vermont's portfolio assessments in 1991-92 and 1992-93. These evaluations concentrated on the reliability of the ratings of the portfolios. In simplest terms, did different evaluators rate the same pupil in the same way? And did evaluators consistently rank different aspects of each pupil's work? In the first year of evaluation, which corresponded to the first year of statewide implementation, reliability was very low on both mathematics and writing. As shown in the table, the correlation of writing scores between different portfolio raters was only 0.6, although that for mathematics reached a more acceptable 0.8.

Writing			*Mathematics*	
Grade	*1991-92*	*1992-93*	*1991-92*	*1992-93*
Fourth	0.49	0.56	0.60	0.72
Eighth	0.60	0.63	0.53	0.79

High rater reliability is, however, a minimal requirement for good assessments. The right things must be measured. The overall congruence of portfolio scores with the desired outcomes for mathematics and writing is unknown. This issue, validity of the assessments, was not fully evaluated because of the low reliability of the scores.

The Vermont experience shows that widespread use of portfolios appears administratively feasible. It does come at a cost: ten to fifteen hours of classroom time a month go into developing portfolios, significant teacher preparation also occurs, and other direct resource expenditures for training and evaluation are required. Part of this time is clearly spent on legitimate student learning activities, but part represents a true additional burden on the teachers and on the class time of the students.

The Vermont experience also demonstrates that classroom instruction can be integrated with the assessment system. The amount of time required to train teachers to use the system is likely to be sizable, however. Further, explicit definition of what is desired is a necessary precursor to obtaining changes.

The assessment experiment has yet to demonstrate whether it is cost-effective Furthermore, the program was not designed to assess individual student performance, and whether it can do this is unknown. As the program is currently structured, unraveling information about the value added of schools or programs appears impossible

Sources: Koretz and others (1993a, 1993b and 1993c).

and analytical ability that have been shown to fit into standardized testing approaches.

Other Performance Measures

Although measures of cognitive skills are a central element in assessing the performance of schools, other important measures include a school's graduation rate, the percentage of graduates that attend post secondary schooling, and the job prospects of graduates. Schools are also expected to develop important social values.

Although they should not be ignored, schools' contributions to progress toward these other objectives is profoundly hard to measure. Specifically, it is very difficult to separate the effects of the school and its teachers from other factors. For example, family income strongly influences college attendance. Changing admission and financial aid policies of colleges and of governments lead to changes in college attendance over time, even when schools provide the same training. Similarly, the strength of local economies influences whether students continue in school or seek employment. Separating the influence of schools from factors outside the control of schools is more difficult in these areas than it is for tests.

Similarly difficult is identifying which specific programs and teachers were instrumental in developing particular skills that are observed only after the student has left school. Because supplying labor markets with better-skilled workers is a primary reason for improving skills, identifying the educational programs that best prepared students for the world of work would be useful but it is seldom possible. The inability to link programs to actual outcomes prevents long-term measurements of the effect of schooling from being used to evaluate specific educational policies. Although useful in setting goals for preparing students for subsequent careers, alternative measures are not now capable of assessing the performance of the school system.

National Standards and Testing

During the past decade, increased emphasis has been put on developing national goals for student performance and on ways to test whether these goals are being met. Together these efforts define minimum, but high performance objectives for graduating students a national consensus of expectations for the achievements of students and schools. And by creating such a consensus, the promoters of national standards hope to remedy one of the identified shortcomings of educational policy: that schools and teachers do not know exactly what is expected of students and, thus, of them.

The best example of the development of national standards is found in mathematics, where mathematics educators have developed specific goals for student achievement (box 13-3). What they have not yet produced, however, is a technique for measuring progress toward those goals. Nor does anyone yet know how instruction might ultimately change as teachers and schools attempt to meet these goals.

Not surprisingly, efforts to create national standards for schools have proved controversial. Apart from concerns about the validity of testing associated with national standards, one of the primary arguments against national testing is that it will reduce local control of schools. If national standards are imposed and if testing relates to these national goals, so the argument goes, local districts will have no choice but to follow the national notions of what schools should be doing, instead of meeting standards laid down by local

Box 7-3. Standards and Testing—The Math Experience

Along with demand for improvement in overall learning has come a call for new, challenging standards of performance. So far the most developed and most acclaimed—effort to develop specific standards for education has been in mathematics. The Mathematical Sciences Education Board of the National Research Council (MSEB) and the National Council of Teachers of Mathematics (NCTM) have collaborated since the mid-1980s to produce several, increasingly detailed reports on specific content standards for mathematics at different levels.

Experience with mathematics standards illustrates several important issues. The MSEB has developed three general principles for linking assessment to effective education: the content principle (assessment should reflect the mathematics that is most important to learn); the learning principle (assessment should enhance mathematics learning and support good instructional practice); and the equity principle (assessment should support every student's opportunity to learn important mathematics). Throughout, the development of standards has been linked to the development do measurements.

But there is a snag. Beyond general principles, linking content standards to measurement is very difficult. Papers commissioned by the MSEB suggest that no one has yet developed accurate methods for assessing whether students are meeting the package of mathematics standards. Furthermore, there is no assurance that instruction will change so that students can be expected to learn what they need to know to meet the standards. Lynn Hancock and Jeremy Kilpatrick review analyses of how testing affects instruction. Although many suggest that "what you test is what you get" that is to say, teachers will spend a large part of class time simply preparing students for the test the evidence is less clear. Students always learn more than is tested and do not learn everything that is tested. Stephen Dunbar and Elizabeth Witt offer a further caution about testing and assessment linked to new standards. Expanded standards for mathematics, they argue, raise new questions about the reliability and validity of existing methods of measurement.

The experiences of those developing mathematics standards and assessments lead to two conclusions. First, it is possible to develop much more specific and appealing definitions of desired learning outcomes than currently exist. Second, the hope of assessment-driven reform of schools is overly optimistic, because existing methods of assessment are not advanced enough for the task and because new methods take considerable time to develop. Improved assessments will continue to be an important element of program evaluations, but they are unlikely by themselves to lead to sufficient changes in teacher incentives and behavior.

Sources: National Research Council (1993); Hancock and Kilpatrick (1993); Dunbar and Witt (1993)

school boards and parents. Such concerns seem overstated. Although local control is portrayed as the historical norm, in fact local control of schools has been steadily eroding for some time. State governments in particular, but also the federal government, already impose goals, curricula, and even details of instructional programs on local districts. The National Assessment of Educational Progress, a continuing effort to measure performance at different ages for a representative group of U.S. students, is in essence a form of national testing that has existed for two decades, and the SAT and Advanced Placement tests can be considered de facto national examinations for college-bound students.

A great deal of local control of education is clearly essential, particularly if performance incentives are to be emphasized. But local control need not, and should not, extend to modifying or overriding minimal goals for student performance set nationally. Students must compete in a national, if not international, market for jobs. In promoting economic development and social mobility, the nation has a legitimate claim to set minimal goals for all students to compete in this national job market.

Less conflict occurs in fact between national goals and local control than would seem the case at first glance. Under most reform plans local districts would be responsible for developing specific educational approaches, designing incentive systems, and meeting the special needs of local populations. But the idea that each locality should follow its own approach to education does not conflict with the idea that the students attending these schools should all reach a standard, minimum level of achievement, nor do national minimum standards prevent localities from developing their own, more stringent standards.

A less high-minded reason for opposing calls for national testing is the reluctance of some school officials to have comparisons made among schools. This concern is justified to the extent that schools are unfairly held responsible for things outside their control. But if national examinations were designed to permit the unraveling of the value added by schools, comparisons would be reasonable and beneficial. Only if school performance in areas agreed to be important is accurately measured can education make progress.

National measurement of achievement is threatened not only by outright opposition, but by indifference and by attempts to divert the energies now focused on measuring performance into national programs to increase educational resources and inputs. Many school officials do not see much use in national standards and testing, because individual districts are more concerned about their own specific programs and student performance than about comparisons with other districts and students. They are thus prone to argue that money spent on national tests would better be spent on actual delivery of educational services.

To complement national performance standards, some propose "opportunity to learn" standards, which would establish national minimum levels for the resources used in teaching students. Such standards would be not only unhelpful, but also potentially damaging. Today's tenuous understanding of the links between school resources and performance make it impossible to define precisely what resources would be needed in a given situation to achieve the national educational goals. So resource standards are likely to promote further inefficiency through mandating inappropriate resources. More insidious, some see this movement as delaying the development of good measures of actual school performance.

Evaluation Approaches and Randomized Assignment Experimentation

In theory, the quality of schooling can be assessed simply by comparing the performance of students in one program with otherwise identical students in different programs. The problem, of course, is that there are no "otherwise identical" students; students and circumstances very across programs in complicated ways. Nonetheless, programs can be evaluated by using statistical methods that combine a wide range of information on students and their schools to isolate the key differences in programs through detailed description of all the separate factors. Applying these statistical approaches correctly is the trick.

The bulk of information about programs, incentive structures, and the like necessarily comes from direct analysis of the programs as they are operated by individual schools. Variations in school districts provide a rich array of experiences. States can work with several school districts, or even schools within a single district, to try deliberately to test all interesting variations of the details of programs and incentive mechanisms. This approach can deepen the schools' understanding of the factors affecting school performance by showing how changes in program details affect overall results.

Schools should also make greater use of an alternative approach, randomized assignment experimentation, which is a method for separating the effect of a specific aspect of treatment from other factors. Medical researchers have made great advances through such experimentation, even when they do not completely understand the underlying physiology of given treatments. The idea is simple in concept but frequently difficult to carry out reliably. The key element is selecting students for specific programs entirely by chance. If done properly, the only systematic influence on performance between those in one program and those in an other will be the program itself.

Suppose, for example, that one wants to study the effect of smaller classes on student achievement. If researchers simply look at performance in the large and small classes found in a typical district, they cannot be sure whether any observed differences in student performance come from the effects of class size or from the specific students and teachers in the different classrooms. For example, if the school principal attempted systematically to provide small classes for the students performing at the lowest level, performance might appear to be lower in the smaller classes, even though that is actually not an effect of the smaller classes per se. To oversome such problems, students (and teachers) could be randomly assigned to classrooms with varying numbers of students, which would reduce the chance that preexisting performance differences would bias measurements of performance by class size. The STAR program in Tennessee used this approach and found further evidence of the general ineffectiveness of smaller classes (box 13-4).

Box 13-4. Project STAR

The Tennessee state legislature funded an unprecedented school experiment in 1985 relating to class size. Early reviews by Gene Glass and Mary Lee Smith of the effects of class size on student performance suggested that reducing class size produces only minimal benefits until classes shrink to fifteen students or fewer a teacher. Before investing in a costly policy of reducing class sizes, Tennessee decided to commission its own study of the effectiveness of smaller classes.

The program, named STAR for "Student/Teacher Achievement Ratio," was a four-year randomized experiment. Students in seventy-nine schools across the state were randomly assigned to a small class (13-17) students), a regular class (22-25 students), or a regular class with a full-time aide. The experiment included students in kindergarten and trades one through three, and participating schools had to have enough students to have each type of classroom. At the end of each grade, students were given Stanford Achievement Tests in reading, math, listening, and word study skills; at the end of grades one through three, they also took the state's Basic Skills First (BSF) test of reading and math.

The results indicate that students in small classes perfom better than those in large classes for kindergarten and perhaps for the first grade. In the second and third grades, small classes made no difference in achievement, after allowing for the initial achievement differences at the end of kindergarten. Students in regular-size classes with aides did not perform significantly better aides did not perform significantly better than classes without aides.

The STAR program illustrates the type of experiment that can uncover information about basic organizational issues. The randomized experiments, which involved selecting a random set of students and assigning a random teacher to each type of classroom attempts to overcome any unmeasured differences among students and treasured differences among students and teachers that might distort achievement gains.

The experiment also illustrates the difficulties of such experimentation. The initial differences in kindergarten achievement could reflect important gains from the use of small classes in the earliest grades, but, because students were not tested at the time of their initial assignment, the differences could also reflect problems with the random assignment of students. The results were probably also limited because achievement differences among students in classes of fifteen would still be fairly small (according to Glass and Smith), compared with those in larger classes. Finally, experimental difficulties associated with student mobility and with the participants' knowledge of the experiment have unknown effects on the results.

The experiment cost about $3 million a year. This amount, while large in terms of evaluation projects, is small compared with the costs of reducing class size in the state. For example, in 1987, Tennessee had 42,000 teachers. If reducing class sizes from twenty-two to fifteen required hiring 30 percent more teachers, the additional one-year salary costs would be $ 300 million (not counting any fringe benefits). If just elementary school class sizes were reduced, the added annual cost would still be close to $200 million. The results of the STAR experiment suggest that most of these additional expenditures would be wasted.

Sources: Glass and Smith (1979); Word and others (1990)

The STAR example also highlights some of the potential difficulties with randomized experimentation. To be appropriate for random assignment experimentation, the program or educational intervention must be well defined and capable of being replicated in many different settings. Class size is appropriate for such experimentation, because variations in size are easy to define and because even fairly small districts have sufficient numbers of classes so that variations in size can be introduced. Conversely, the effect of state teacher certification requirements, say, in the number of courses in pedagogy that are required of prospective teachers, is difficult to evaluate using randomized assignment because the certification requirements apply across an entire state; changing requirements for individual districts would interact with the hiring practices of those districts, making any observed effects difficult to interpret. Additionally, educational experiments are bedeviled by student mobility. The full effects of educational programs generally take some time to evolve, but maintaining randomly assigned programs for students who have moved to a new district or observing their achievement as they progress through school is difficult. Thus, randomized experiments are an appropriate and valuable tool that should be used more extensively, but they cannot be the only method of evaluation.

Because of the technical, theoretical, and political difficulties of more comprehensive evaluations of school performance, undertaking testing programs is a task that only the largest and most sophisticated school districts may be able to do on their own. So the higher levels of government have a clear role to play.

Governmental Responsibilities

State and federal governments, like local school districts, exhibit a distinct lack of enthusiasm for evaluating schools even though from their broader perspective they would seem to have much more incentive to do so than districts, which have always focused on educating students. These governments have done only limited amounts of systematic analysis and evaluation. Traditionally the federal government has undertaken sufficient evaluation only to justify reauthorization of its primary programs, such as compensatory education funding or Head Start. It has done little in areas outside of the programs it funds. States themselves have not taken on a very broad role in evaluation.

The task of developing and providing information about alternative educational approaches should be part of the primary mission of federal and state education departments. Knowledge about the performance of specific programs of incentive plans can help to guide the decisions of all districts in the country. Many approaches that involve substantially different operating procedures cannot be fully evaluated by looking at only a single district. And the complexity of the educational process itself makes evaluation of even simple programs difficult. Highly skilled and specialized personnel are often required if an evaluation is to be done properly, and most local districts will not, and generally should not, attempt to develop complete evaluation offices. Each of these factors bolsters the case for state and federal provision of evaluation services. State and federal education agencies should also disseminate the results of the evaluations. These agencies are in a position to see a broad range of options. They also can produce the relevant information for broad groups of consumers.

Nonetheless, two obstacles stand in the way of a more productive government role in the evaluation of education. First, local districts are not always eager to have state and federal officials involved in local activities. Second, as described previously, the most useful long-run information will come from observing the outcomes of a variety of organizational structures and incentive programs. Although some variation in incentive structures might happen naturally across districts, it most likely would not be varied sufficiently to provide precise information about effectiveness. Each of these difficulties will call for a new compact between state and local districts, which will need to cooperate more fully in designing and evaluating innovative incentive programs. Inducements to persuade local districts to cooperate may be necessary. The districts may find participation in experimental programs too difficult or time-consuming, and they may be unwilling to risk having ineffective programs exposed. Reversing those traditional attitudes on the part of local districts is one of the challenges and necessities of reform.

The Burden of Testing and Evaluation

Although the potential benefits of more comprehensive testing generate considerable enthusiasm, the burden of testing and evaluating creates considerable concern. Testing students takes time, and schools frequently express doubts about whether additional testing would be worth the time and money. Current testing programs do not appear to be excessive; an average of fewer than four hours a year is spent in testing for all students, although testing for some students in some years can get noticeably larger. As with all other forms of educational expenditure, testing is justified only when the benefits exceed the costs.

Today, school districts can and should use tests directly to help with the selection, design, and reform of educational programs. Testing could also provide more and better information about the results of programs from other districts. Future testing should be done with a specific purpose, and testing programs should themselves be evaluated by state and federal governments. Used more diligently and intelligently, testing could become not a burden, but the foundation of a program of experimentation and learning to educate educators about education: what works, what does not, and what could work better. Such a program offers the United States its best hope of comprehensive education reform.

Information for Parents

It is common to lament the fact that parents are not more actively involved in the schools and that some do not show much interest in their children's education. One reason for this parental neglect is the minimal amount of information parents ever receive about schools, parents have little hope of making informed judgments about the quality of alternative schools or programs. Without more and better information. parents cannot participate effectively in school decisions, even at the level of voting for school budgets.

Improved school evaluation could provide parents with the information they need. Indeed, some reforms would require parents to have better information and to participate more actively in schooling. For example, school choice programs would not work if parents had to make choices based only on currently available information. Without better information about performance and achievement across schools, choices would likely revolve around issues of race and social status pushing the results of choice programs in very undesirable directions.

Institutional Learning

Schools invest remarkably little in information about their own operations. Compared with that on private industry, the amount of research and development on schools is minute. So also is the amount of resources and energy devoted to quality assurance in schools. More than that, school personnel are accustomed to think that evaluation of programs and activities is unimportant, more a nuisance than a necessity.

In contrast to teacher' own behavior, this attitude is even more remarkable. Teachers continually evaluate their students, knowing that such information is invaluable in determining whether a student is meeting objectives, having difficulties with material, working sufficiently hard, and being properly prepared for the future. Teachers have few qualms about evaluating students in areas where objective measurement is exceedingly difficult, from social skills to attitudes.

Schools themselves must actively learn; continuing the unchecked drift of the past quarter century is simply untenable, Schools, like their students, must be subjected to systematic measurement and evaluation. The information generated by this process must in turn be employed to direct the course of development of the schools.

14

The Consequences of Literacy

The accepted tripartite divisions of the formal study both of mankind's past and present are to a considerable extent based on man's development first of language and later of writing. Looked at in the perspective of time, man's biological evolution shades into prehistory when he becomes a language-using animal; add writing, and history proper begins. Looked at in a temporal perspective, man as animal is studied primarily by the zoologist, man as talking animal primarily by the anthropologist, and man as talking and writing animal primarily by the sociologist.

That the differentiations between these categories should be founded on different modes of communication is clearly appropriate; it was language that enabled man to achieve a form of social organisation whose range and complexity was different in kind from that of animals: whereas the social organisation of animals was mainly instinctive and genetically transmitted, that of man was largely learned and transmitted verbally through the cultural heritage. The basis for the last two distinctions, those based on the development of writing, is equally clear: to the extent that a significant quantity of written records are available the pre-historian yields to the historian; and to the extent that alphabetical writing and popular literacy imply new modes of social organisation and transmission, the anthropologist tends to yield to the sociologist.

But why? And how? There is no agreement about this question, nor even about what the actual boundary lines between non-literate and literate cultures are. At what point in the formalization of pictographs or other graphic signs can we talk of "letter," of literacy ? And what proportion of the society has to write and read before the culture as a whole can be described as literate ?

These are some of the many reasons why the extent to which there is any distinction between the areas and methods peculiar to anthropology and sociology must be regarded as problematic; and the difficulty affects not only the boundaries of the two disciplines but also the nature of the intrinsic difference in their subject matter. The recent trend has been for anthropologists to spread their net more widely and engage in the study of industrial societies side by side with their sociological, colleagues. We can no longer accept the view that anthropologists have as their objective the study of primitive man, who is characterised by a "primitive mind,"while sociologists, on the other hand, concern themselves with civilised man, whose activities are guided by "rational thought" and tested by "logico-empirical procedures." The reaction against such ethnocentric views, however, has now gone to the point of denying that the distinction between non-literate society has any significant validity. This position seems contrary to our personal observation; and so it has seemed worthwhile to enquire whether there may not be, even from the most empirical and relativist standpoint, genuine illumination to be derived from a further consideration of some of the historical and analytic problems connected with the traditional dichotomy between non-literate and literate societies.

1. The Cultural Tradition in Non-Literate Societies

For reasons which will become clear it seems best to begin with a generalised description of the ways in which the cultural heritage is transmitted in non-literate societies,and then to see how these ways are changed by the widespread adoption of an easy and effective means of written communication.

When one generation hands on its cultural heritage to the next, three fairly separate items are involved. First, the society passes on its material plant, including the natural resources available to its members. Secondly, it transmits standardised ways of acting. These customary ways of behaving are only party communicated by verbal means; ways of cooking food, of growing crops, of handling children may be transmitted by direct imitation. But the most significant elements of any human culture are undoubtedly chanelled through words, and reside in the particular range of meanings and attitudes which members of any society attach to their verbal symbols. These elements include not only what we habitually think of as customary behavior but also such items as ideas of space and time, generalised goals and aspirations, in short the *weltanschauung* of every social group. In Durkheim's words, these categories of the understanding are "priceless" instruments of thought which the human groups have laboriously forged through the centuries and where they have accumulated the best of their intellectual capital." The relative continuity of these categories of understanding from one generation to another is primarily ensured by language, which is the most direct and comprehensive expression of the social experience of the group.

The transmission of the verbal elements of culture by oral means can be visualised as a long chain of interlocking conversations between members of the group. Thus all beliefs and values, all forms of knowledge, are communicated between individuals in face-to-face contact; and, as distinct from the material content of the cultural transition, whether it be cave-paintings to handaxes, they are stored only in human memory.

The intrinsic nature of oral communication has a considerable effect upon both the content and the transmission of the cultural repertoire. In the first place it makes for a directness of relationship between symbol and referent. There can be no reference to "dictionary definitions," nor can words accumulate the successive layers of historically validated meanings which they acquire in a literate culture. Instead the meaning of each word is ratified in a succession of concrete situations, accompanied by vocal inflexions and physical gestures, all of which combine to particularize both its specific denotation and its accepted connotative usages. This process of direct semantic ratification, of course, operates cumulatively; and as a result the totality of symbol-referent relationships is more immediately experienced by the individual in an exclusively oral culture, and is thus more deeply socialized.

One way of illustrating this is to consider how the range of vocabulary in a non-literate society reflects this mode of semantic ratification. It has often been observed how the elaboration of the vocabulary of such a society reflects the particular interests of the people concerned. The inhabitants of the Pacific island of Lesu have not one, but a dozen or so, words for pigs, according to sex, color, and where they come from—a prolixity which mirrors the importance of pigs in a domestic economy that otherwise includes few sources of protein. The corollary of this prolixity is that where common emphases and interests, whether material or otherwise, are not specifically involved, there is little verbal development. Malinowski reported that in the Trobriands the outer world was only named insofar as it yielded useful things, useful, that is, in the very broadest sense; and there is much other testimony to support the view that there is an intimate functional adaptation of language in non-literate societies, which obtains not only for the relatively simple and concrete symbol-referents involved avbove, but also for the more generalized "categories of understanding" and for the cultural tradition as a whole.

In an essay he wrote in collaboration with Mauss, "De quelques formes primitives de classifications," Durkheim traces the interconnections between the ideas of space and the territorial distribution of the Australian aborigines, the Zuni of the Pueblo area and the Sioux of the Great Plains. This intermeshing of what he called the collective representations with the social morphology of a particular society is clearly another aspect of the same directness of relationship between symbol and referent. Just as the more concrete part of a vocabulary reflects the dominant interests of the society, so the more abstract categories are often closely linked to the accepted terminology for pragmatic pursuits. Among the LoDagaa of Northern Ghana, days are reckoned according to the incidence of neighboring markets; the very word for day and market is the same, and the "weekly" cycle is a six-day revolution of the most important markets in the vicinity, a cycle which also defines the spatial range of everyday activities.

The way in which these various institutions in an oral culture are kept in relatively close accommodation one to another surely bears directly on the question of the central difference between literate and non-literate societies. As we have remarked, the whole content of the social tradition, apart from the material inheritances, is held in memory. The social aspects of remembering have been emphasised by sociologists and psychologists, in particular Maurice Halbwachs.[7] What the individual remembers tends to be what is of critical importance in his experience of the main social relationships. In each generation, therefore, the individual memory will mediate the cultural heritage in such a way that its new constituents will adjust to the old by the process of interpretation that Bartlett calls "rationalizing" or the "effort after meaning"; and whatever parts of it have ceased to be of contemporary relevance are likely to be eliminated by the process of forgetting.

The social function of memory—and of forgetting—can thus be seen as the final stage of what may be called the homeostatic organisation of the cultural tradition in non-literate society. The language is developed in intimate association with the experience of the community, and it is learned by the individual in face-to-face contact with the other members. What continues to be of social relevance is stored in the memory while the rest is usually forgotten: and language—primarily vocabulary—is the effective medium of this crucial process of social digestion and elimination which may be regarded as analogous to the homeostatic organisation of the human body by means of which it attempts to maintain its present condition of life.

In drawing attention to the importance of these assimilating mechanisms in non-literate societies, we are denying neither the occurrence of social change, nor yet the "survivals" which it leaves in its wake. Nor do we overlook the existence of mnemonic devices in oral cultures which offer some resistance to the interpretative process. Formalised patterns of speech, recital under ritual conditions, the use of drums and other musical instruments, the employments of professional remembrancers—all such factors may shield at least part of the content of memory from the transmuting influence of the immediate pressures of the present. The Homeric epics, for instance, seem to have been written down during the first century of Greek literature between 750 and 650 B.C., but "they look to a departed era, and their substance is unmistakably old."

With these qualifications, however, it seems correct to characterize the transmission of the cultural tradition in oral societies as homeostatic in view of the way in which its emphasis differs from that in literate societies. The description offered has, of course, been extremely abstract; but a few illustrative examples in one important area—that as how the tribal past is digested into the communal orientation of the present—may serve to make it clearer.

Like the Bedouin Arabs and the Hebrews of the Old Testament, the Tiv people of Nigeria give long genealogies of their forebears which in this case stretch some twelve generations in depth back to an eponymous founding ancestor. Neither these genealogies, not the Biblical lists of the descendents of Adam, were remembered purely as feats of memory. They served as mnemonics for systems of social relations. When on his deathbed Jacob delivered prophecies about the future of his twelve sons, he spoke of them as the twelve tribes or nations of Israel. It would seem from the account in Genesis that the genealogical tables here refer to contemporary groups rather than to dead individuals; the tables presumably serve to regulate social relations among the twelve tribes of Israel in a manner similar to that which has been well analysed in Evans-Pritchard's work on the Nuer of the Southern Sudan and in Fortes' account of the Tallensi of Northern Ghana.

Early British administrators among the Tiv of Nigeria were aware of the great importance attached to these genealogies, which were continually discussed in court cases where the rights and duties of one man towards another were in dispute. Consequently they took the trouble to write down the long lists of names and preserve them for posterity, so that future administrators might refer to them in giving judgement. Forty years later, when the Bohannans carried ourt anthropological field work in the area, their successors were still using the same genealogies. However, these written pedigrees now gave rise to many disagreements; the Tiv maintained that they were incorrect, while the officials regarded them as statements of fact, as records of what had actually happened, and could not agree that the unlettered indigenes could be better informed about the past than their own literate predecessors. What neither party realised was that in any society of this kind changes take place which require a constant readjustment in the genealogies if they are to continue to carry out their function as mnemonics of social relationships.

These changes are of several kinds: those arising from the turnover in personnel from the process of "birth and copulation and death", those connected with the rearrangement of the constituent units of the society with the migration of one group and the fission of another; and lastly those resulting from the effects of changes in the social system itself, whether generated from within or initiated from without. Each of these three processes (which we may refer to for convenience as the processes of generational, organisational and structural change) could lead to alterations of the kind to which the administration objected.

It is obvious that the process of generation leads in itself to a constant lengthening of the genealogy; on the other hand, the population to which it is linked may in fact be growing at quite a different rate, perhaps simply replacing itself. So despite its increasing length the genealogy may have to refer to just as many people at the present time as it did fifty, a hundred, or perhaps two hundred years ago. Consequently the added depth of lineages caused by new births needs to be accompanied by a process of genealogical shrinkage; the occurrence of this telescoping process, a common example of the general social phenomenon which J. A. Barnes has felicitously termed "structural amnesia," has been attested in many societies, including all those mentioned above.

Organisational changes lead to similar adjustments. The state of Gonja in Northern Ghana is divided into a number of divisional chiefdoms, certain of which are recognised as providing in turn the ruler of the whole nation. When asked to explain their system the Gonja recount how the founder of the state, Ndewura Jakpa, came down from the Niger Bend in search of gold, conquered, the indigenous inhabitants of the area and enthroned himself as chief of the state and his sons as rulers of its territorial divisions. At his death the divisional chiefs succeeded to the paramountcy in turn. When the details of this story were first recorded at the turn of the present century, at the time the British were extending their control over the area, Jakpa was said to have begotten seven sons, this corresponding to the number of divisions whose heads were eligible for the supreme office by virtue of their descent from the founder of the particular chiefdom. But at the same time as the British had arrive, two of the seven divisions disappeared, one being deliberately incorporated in a neighboring division because its rulers had supported a Mandingo invader, Samori, and another because of some boundary changes introduced by the British administration. Sixty years later when the myths of state were again recorded, Jakpa was credited with only five sons and no mention was made of the founders of the two divisions which had since disappeared form the political map.

These two instances from the Tiv and the Gonja emphasise that genealogies often serve the same function that Malinowski claimed for myth; they act as "charters" of present social institutions rather than as faithful historical records of times past. They can do this more consistently because they operate within an oral rather than a written tradition and thus tend to be automatically adjusted to existing social relations as they are passed by word of mouth from one member of the society to another. The social element in remembering results in the genealogies being transmuted in the course of being transmitted; and a similar process takes place with regard to other cultural elements as well, to myths, for example, and to sacred lore in general. Deities and other supernatural agencies which have served their purpose can be quietly dropped from the contemporary pantheon; and as the society changes, myths too are forgotten, attributed to other personages, or transformed in their meaning.

One of the most important results of this homeostatic tendency is that the individual has little perception of the past except in terms of the present; whereas the annals of a literate society cannot but enforce a more objective recognition of the distinction between what was and what is. Franz Boas wrote that for the Eskimo the world has always been it is now: it seems probable, at least, that the form in which nonliterate societies conceive the world of the past is itself influenced by the process of transmission described. The Tiv have their genealogies, others their sacred tales about the origin of the world and the way in which man acquired his culture. But all their conceptualisations of the past cannot help being governed by the concerns of the present, merely because there is no body of chronologically ordered statements to which reference can be made. The Tiv do not recognise any contradiction between what they say nor and what they said fifty years ago, since no enduring records exist for them to set beside their present views. Myth and history merge into one: the elements in the cultural heritage which cease to have a contemporary relevance tend to be soon forgotten or transformed; and as the individuals of each generation acquire their vocabulary, their genealogies, and their myths, they are unaware that various words proper-names and stories have dropped out, or that others have changed their meanings or been replaced.

II. Kinds Of Writing And Their Social Effects

The pastness of the past, then, depends upon a historical sensibility which can hardly begin to operate without permanent written records; and writing introduces similar changes in the transmission of other items of the cultural repertoire. But the extent of these changes varies with the nature and social distribution of the writing system; varies, that is, according to the system's intrinsic efficacy as a means of communication, and accoridng to the social constraints placed upon it, that is the degree to which use of the system is diffused through the society.

Early in prehistory man began to express himself in graphic from; and his cave paintings, rock engravings and wood carvings are morphologically and presumably sequentially, the forerunners of writing. By some process of simplification and stylisation they appear to have led to the various kinds of pictographs found in simple societies. While pictographs themselves are almost universal, their development into a self-sufficient system capable of extended discourse occurs only among the Plains Indians.

Pictographs have obvious disadvantages as means of communication. For one thng a vast number of signs is needed to represent all the important objects in the culture. For another, since the signs are concrete, the simplest sentence requires an extremely elaborate series of signs: many stylised representations of wigwams, footprints, totemic animals and so on are required just to convey the information that a particular man left there a few days ago. Finally, however elaborately the system is developed only a limited number of things can be said.

The end of the fourth millennium saw the early stages of the development of more complex forms of writing, which seem to be an essential factor in the rise of the urban cultures of the Orient. The majority of signs in these systems were simply pictures of the outside would, standardised representations of the object signified by a particular word; to these were added other devices for creating word signs or logograms, which permitted the expression of wider ranges of meaning. Thus in Egyptian hieroglyphics the picture of a beetle was a code-sign not only for that insect but also for a discontinuous and more abstract referent "became".

The basic invention used to supplement the logograms was the phonetic principle, which for the first time permitted the written expression of all the words of a language. For example, by the device of phonetic transfer the Sumerians could use the sign for *ti* an arrow, to stand for life, a concept not easy to express in pictographic form. In particular, the need to record personal names and foreign words encouraged the development of phonetic elements in writing.

But while these true writing systems all used phonetic devices for the construction of logograms (and have consequently been spoken of as word-syllabic systems of writing), they failed to carry through the application of the phonetic principle exclusively and systematically. The achievement of a system completely based upon the representation of phonemes (the basic units of meaningful sound) was left to the Near Eastern syllabaries, which developed between 1500-1000 B.C., and finally to the introduction of the alphabet proper in Greece. Meanwhile these incompletely phonetic system were too clumsy and complicated to foster widespread literacy, if only because the number of sings was very large; at least six hundred would have to be learned even for the simplified cuneiform developed in Assyria, and about the same for Egyptian hieroglyphs. All these ancient civilisations, the Sumerian, Egyptian, Hittite and Chinese, were literate in one sense and their great advances in administration and technology were undoubtedly connected with the invention of a writing system; but when we think of the limitations of their systems of communication as compared with ours, the term "protoliterate" or even "oligoliterate," might be more descriptive in suggesting the restriction of literacy to a relatively small proportion of the total population.

Any system of writing which makes the sign stand directly for the object must be extremely complex. It can extend its vocabulary by generalisation or association of ideas, that is, by making the sign stand either for a more general class of objects, or for other referents connected with the original picture by an association of meanings which may be related to one another either in a continuous or in a discontinuous manner. Either process of semantic extension is to some extent arbitrary or esoteric; and as a result the interpretation of these signs is neither easy nor explicit. One might perhaps guess that the Chinese sign for a man carries the general meaning of maleness; it would be more difficult to see that a conventionalised picture of a man and a broom is the sign for a woman; it's pleasing fancy, no doubt, but not one which communicates very readily until it has been learned as a new character, as a separate sign for a separate word, as a logogram. In Chinese writing a minimum of

3000 such characters have to be learned before one can be reasonably literate; and with a total repertoire of some 50,000 characters to be mastered, it normally takes about twenty years to reach full literate proficiency. China, therefore, stands as an extreme example of how, when a virtually nonphonetic system of writing becomes sufficiently developed to express a large number of meanings explicitly, only a small and specially trained professional group in the total society can master it, and partake of the literate culture.

Although system of word signs are certainly easier to learn, many difficulties remain, even when these sings are supplemented by phonemic devices of a syllabic sort. Other features of the social system are no doubt responsible for the way that the writing systems developed as they did: but it is a striking fact that—for whatever ultimate causes—in Egypt and Mesopotamia, as in China, a literate elite of religious administrative and commercial experts emerged and maintained itself as a centralised governing bureaucracy on rather similar lines. Their various social and intellectual achievements were, of course, enormous; but as regards the participation of the society as a whole in the written culture, a wide gap existed between the esoteric literate culture and the exoteric oral one, a gap which the literate were interested in maintaining. Among the Sumerians and Akkadians writing was the pursuit of scribes and preserved as a "mystery," a 'secret treasure." Royalty were themselves illiterate; Ashurbanipal (668-626 B.C.) records that he was the first Babylonian king to master the "clerkly skill." "Put writing in your heart that you may protect yourself from hard labour of any kind", writes an Egyptian of the New Kingdom: "The scribe is released from manual tasks;" it is he who commands." Significantly, the classical age of Babylonian culture, beginning under Hammurabi in the late eighteenth century B.C. appears to have coincided with a period when the reading and writing of Akkadian cuneiform was not confined to a small group nor to one nation; it was then that nearly all the extant literature was written down, and that the active state of commerce and administration produced a vast quantity of public and private correspondence, of which much has survived.

These imperfectly phonetic methods of writing survived with little change for many centuries; so too did the cultures of which they were part. The existence of an elite group, which followed form the difficulty of the writing system, and whose continued influence depended on the maintenance of the present social order, must have been a powerfully conservative force, especially when it consisted of ritual specialists; and so, it may be surmised, was the nature of the writing system itself. For pictographic and logographic systems are alike in their tendency to reify the objects of the natural and social order; by so doing they register, record, make permanent the existing social and ideological picture. Such for example, was the tendency of the most highly developed and longest-lived ancient writing system, that of Egypt, whose society has been described with picturesque exaggeration as "a nation of fellahin ruled with a rod of iron by a Society of Antiquaries."

This conservative or antiquarian bias can perhaps be best appreciated by contrasting it with fully phonetic writing; for phonetic writing by imitating human discourse, is in fact symbolising, not the objects of the social and natural order, but the very process of human interaction in speech; the verb is as easy to express as the noun; and the written vocabulary can be easily and unambiguously expanded. Phonetic systems are therefore adapted to expressing every nuance of individual thought to recording personal reactions as well as items of major social importance. Non-phonetic writing, on the other hand, tends rather to record and reify only those items in the cultural repertoire which the literate specialists have selected for written expression; and it tends to express the collective attitude towards them.

The notion of representing a sound by a graphic symbol is itself so stupefying a leap of the imagination that what is remarkable is not so much that it happened relatively late in human history, but rather that it ever happened at all. For a long time, however, these phonetic inventions had a limited effect because they were only partially exploited; not only were logograms and pictograms retained but a variety of phonograms were used to express the same sound. The full explicitness and economic of a phonetic writing system "as easy as A B C" was therefore likely to arise only in less advanced societies on the fringes of Egypt or Mesopotamia, societies which were starting their writing system more or less from scratch, and which took over the idea of phonetic signs from adjoining countries and used them exclusively to fit their own language. These phonetic signs could, of course, be used to stand for any unit of speech, and thus developed either into syllabaries or into alphabets. In a few cases, such as Japanese, the particular nature of the language made it possible to construct a relatively simple and efficient syllabary; but as regards the great majority of languages the alphabet, with its signs for individual consonants and vowels, proved a much more economical and convenient instrument for representing sounds. For the syllabaries, while making writing easier, were still far from simple; they were often combined with logograms and pictographs. And whether by necessity or tradition or both, pre-alphabetic writing was still mainly restricted to elite groups. The Mycenean script disappeared completely after the 12th century B.C., a fact which was possible because of the very restricted uses of literacy and the close connection between writing and palace administration. It is doubtful whether any such loss could have occurred in Greece after the introduction of a complete alphabetic script, probably in the eighth century B.C.

The alphabet is almost certainly the supreme example of cultural diffusion: all existing or recorded alphabets derive from Semitic syllabaries developed during the second millennium. Eventually there arose the enormous simplification of the Semitic writing system, with its mere twenty-two letters; and then only one further step remained: the Greek script which is of course, much closer than the Semitic to the Roman alphabet, took certain of the Semitic signs for consonants which the Greek language didn't need, and used them for vowels, which the Semitic syllabary did not represent. The directness of our inheritance from these two sources is suggested by the fact that our word "alphabet" is the latinized form of the first two letters of the Greek alphabet, "alpha," derived from the Semitic "aleph" and "beta" from the Semitic "beth".

The reason for the success of the alphabet, which David Diringer calls a "democratic" script as opposed to the "theocratic" scrips of Egypt, is itself based on the fact that, uniquely among writing systems, its graphic signs are representations of the most extreme and most universal example of cultural selection—the basic phonemic system. The number of sounds which the human breath stream can produce is vast; but nearly all languages are based on the formal recognition by the society of only forty or so of these sounds. The success of the alphabet (as well as some of its incidental difficulties) comes from the fact that its system of graphic representation takes advantage of this socially-conventionalized pattern of sound in all language systems; by symbolizing in letter these selected phonemic units the alphabet makes it possible to write easily and read unambiguously about anything which the society can talk about.

The historical picture of the cultural impact of the new alphabetic writing is not altogether clear. As regards the Semitic system, which was widely adopted elsewhere, the evidence suggests that—in part perhaps because of the intrinsic difficulties of the system, but mainly because of the established cultural features of the societies which adopted it—the social diffusion of writing was slow. There was, for one thing a strong tendency for writing to be used as a help to memory rather than as an autonomous and independent mode of communication; and under such conditions its influence tended towards the consolidation of the existing cultural tradition. This certainly appears to be true to India and Palestine. Gandz notes, for example, that Hebrew culture continued to be transmitted orally long after the Old Testament had begun to be written down. As he puts it, the introduction of writing:

Did not at once change the habits of the people and displace the old method of oral tradition. We must always distinguish between the *first introduction* of writing and its *general diffusion.* It often takes several centuries, and sometimes even a millennium or more until this invention becomes the common property of the people at large. In the beginning, the written book is not intended for practical use at all. It is a divine instrument, placed in the temple "by the side of the ark of the covenant that it may be there for a witness" (Deuteronomy xxxi, 26) and remains there as a holy relic. For the people at large, oral instruction still remained the only way of learning, and the memory—the only means of preservation. Writing was practiced if at all only as an additional support for the memory....

It was not, in fact, until some six centuries after the original Hebrew adoption of the Semitic writing system that, at the time of Ezra (ca. 444 B.C.), an official "generally recognized text" of the Torah was published, and the body of the religious tradition ceased to be "practically...a sealed book" and become accessible to anyone who chose to study it.

Even so, of course, as the frequent diatribes against the scribes in the Gospels remind us, there remained a considerable gap between the literati and the laymen; the professionals who plied their trade in the market-place belonged to "families of scribes," perhaps organized as guilds, within which the mystery was handed down from father to son.

Anything like popular literacy, or the use of writing as an autonomous mode of communication by the majority of the members of society, is not found in the earliest societies which used the Semitic writing system; it was, rather, in the sixth and fifth centuries B.C. in the city states of Greece and Ionia that there first arose a society which as a whole could justly be characterized as literate. Many of the reasons why literacy became widespread in Greece, but not in other societies which had Semitic, or indeed any other, simple and explicit writing systems, necessarily lie outside the scope of this essay; yet considerable importance must surely be attributed to the intrinsic advantages of the Greek adaptation of the Semitic alphabet, an adaptation which made it the first comprehensively and exclusively phonetic system for transcribing human speech. The system was easy, explicit and unambiguous—more so than the Semitic where the lack of vowels is responsible for many of the cruxes in the Bible; for instance, since the consonant in the Hebrew words is the same, Elijah may have been fed by

"Ravens" or "Arabs." Its great advantage over the syllabaries lay in the reduction of the number of signs and in the ability to specify consonant and vowel clusters. The system was easy to learn: Plato sets aside three years for the process in the *Laws,* about the time taken in our schools today; and the much greater speed with which alphabetic writing can be learned is shown, not only by such reports as those of the International Institute of Intellectual Cooperation in 1934, but also by the increasing adoption of the Roman script, and even more widely of alphabetic systems of writing throughout the world.

The extensive diffusion of the alphabet in Greece was also materially assisted by various social economic and technological factors. In the first place the 8th century saw a great burst of economic activity following the revival of the eastern trade which had declined after the Mycenean collapse in the 12th century. Secondly, while the Greek society of the period had, of course, its various social, strata, the political system was not strongly centralized; especially in the Ionic settlements there appears to have been a good deal of flexibility and in them we discern the beginnings of the Greek city state. Thirdly, the increased contact with the East brought material prosperity and technological advance. The wider use of iron, the advent of the true Iron Age, was perhaps one of the results. More closely connected with literacy was the fact that trade with Egypt led to the importation of papyrus; and this made writing itself easier and less expensive, both for the individual writer and for the reader who wanted to buy books: papyrus was obviously much cheaper than parchment made from skins, more permanent than wax tablets easier to handle than the stone or clay of Mesopotamia and Mycenae.

The chronology and extent of the diffusion of literacy in Greece remains a matter of debate. With the Mycenean collapse in the 12th century, writing disappeared; the earliest Greek inscriptions in the modified Semitic alphabet occur in the last two decades of the 8th century. Recent authorities suggest the new script was adopted and transformed about the middle of the 8th century in Northern Syria. The extensive use of writing probably came only slowly in the 7th century, but when it eventually came it seems to have been used in a very wide range of activities intellectual as well as economic and by a wide range of people.

It must be remembered, of course, that Greek writing throughout the classical period was still relatively difficult to decipher, as words were not regularly separated; that the copying of manuscripts was a long and laborious process; and that silent reading as we know it was very rare until the advent of printing—in the ancient world books were used mainly for reading aloud, often by a slave. Nevertheless, from the sixth century onwards literacy seems to be increasingly presumed in the public life of Greece and Ionia. In Athens, for example, the first laws for the general public to read were set up by Solon in 593-4 B.C,; the institution of ostracism early in the fifth century assumes a literate citizen body-6,000 citizens had to write the name of the person on their potsherds before he could be banished; there is abundant evidence in the fifth century of a system of schools teaching reading and writing and of a book-reading public-satirized already by Aristophanes in *The Frogs,* while the final form of the Greek alphabet, which was established fairly late in the fifth century, was finally adopted for us in the official records of Athens by decree of the Archon Eucleides in 403 B.C.

III. Alphabetic Culture And Greek Thought

The rise of Greek civilization, then, is the prime historical example of the transition to a really literate society. In all subsequent cases where a widespread introduction of an alphabetic script occurred, as in Rome, for example, other cultural features were inevitably imported from the loan country along with the writing system; Greece thus offers not only the first example of this change, but also the essential one for any attempt to isolate the cultural consequences of alphabetic literacy.

The fragmentary and ambiguous nature of our direct evidence about this historical transformation in Greek civilization means that any generalizations must be extremely tentative and hypothetical; but the fact that the essential basis both of the writing systems and of many characteristic cultural institutions of the Western tradition as a whole are derived from Greece, and that they both arose there simultaneously, would seem to justify the present attempt to outline the possible relationship between the writing system and those cultural innovations of early Greece which are common to all alphabetically literate societies.

The early development of the distinctive features of Western thought is usually traced back to the radical innovations of the pre-Socratic philosophers of the sixth century B.C. The essence of their intellectual revolution is seen as a change from mythical to logico-empirical modes of thought. Such broadly speaking, is Werner Jaeger's view; and Ernst Cassirer writes that "the history of philosophy as a scientific discipline may be regarded as a single continuous struggle to effect a separation and liberation from myth."

To this general picture there are two kinds of theoretical objection. First, that the crucial intellectual innovations—in Cassirer as in Werner Jaeger—are in the last analysis attributed to the special mental endowments of the Greek people; and insofar as such terms as "the Greek Mind" or "genius" are not simply descriptive, they are logically dependent upon extremely questionable theories of man's nature and culture. Secondly, such a version of the transformation from "unphilosophical" to "philosophical" thought assumes an absolute—and untenable—dichotomy between the "mythical" thought of primitives and the "logico-empirical' thought of civilized man.

The dichotomy, of course, is itself very similar to Levy-Bruhl's earlier theory of the "prelogical" mentality of primitive peoples which has been widely criticised. Malinowski and many others have demonstrated the empirical elements in non-literate cultures and Evans-pritchard has carefully analyzed the "logical" nature of the belief systems of the Azande of the Sudan; while on the other hand the illogical and mythical nature of much Western thought and behavior is evident to anyone contemplating either our past or our present.

Nevertheless, although we must reject any dichotomy based upon the assumption of radical differences between the mental attributes of literate and non-literate peoples, and accept the view that previous formulations of the distinction were based on faulty premises and inadequate evidence, there may still exist general differences between literate and non-literate societies somewhat along the lines suggested by Levy-Bruhl. One reason for their existence, for instance, may be what has been described above; the fact that writing establishes a different kind of relationship between the word and its referent, a relationship that is more general and more abstract, and less closely connected with the particularities of person, place and time, than obtains in oral communication. There is certainly a good deal to substantiate this distinction in what we know of early Greek thought. To take, for instance, the categories of Cassirer and Werner Jaeger, it is surely significant that it was only in the days of the first widespread alphabetic culture that the idea of "logic"—of an immutable and impersonal mode of discourse—appears to have arisen; and it was also onlv then that the sense of the human past as an objective reality was formally developed, a process in which the distinction between "myth' and "history" took on decisive importance.

a. Myth and History

Non-literate peoples, of course, often make a distinction between the lighter folk-tale, the graver myth and the quasi-historical legend.[55] But not so insistently, and for an obvious reason. As long as the legendary and doctrinal aspects of the cultural tradition are mediated orally, they are kept in relative harmony with each other and with the present needs of society in two ways; through the unconscious operations of memory, and through the adjustment of the reciter's terms and attitudes to those of the audience before him. There is evidence, for example, that such adaptations and omissions occurred in the oral transmission of the Greek cultural tradition. But once the poems of Homer and Hesiod, which contained much of the earlier history, religion and cosmology of the Greeks, had been written down, succeeding generations were faced with old distinctions in sharply aggravated form; how far was the information about their Gods and heroes literally true? how could its patent inconsistencies be explained? and how could the beliefs and attitudes implied be brought into line with those of the present?

The disappearance of so many early Greek writings and the difficulties of dating and composition in many that survive, make anything like a clear reconstruction impossible. Greek had of course been written in a very limited way, during Mycenean times. At about 1200 writing disappeared and the alphabet was not developed until some four hundred years later. Most scholars agree that in the middle or late eighth century the Greeks adapted the purely consonantal system of Phoenicia, possibly at the trading port of Mina (Poseidon?). Much of the early writing consisted of "explanatory inscriptions on existing objects—dedications on offerings personal names on property, epitaphs on tombs, names of figures in drawings." The Homeric poems were written down between 750 and 650 B.C., and the seventh century saw first the recording of lyric verse and then (at the end) the emergence of the great Ionian school of scientist philosophers. Thus within a century or two of the witting down of the Homeric poems, many groups of writers and teachers appeared, first in Ionia and later in Greece, who took as their point of departure the belief that much of what Homer had apparently said was inconsistent and unsatisfactory in many respects. The logographers, who set themselves to record the genealogies, chronologies and cosmologies which had been handed down orally from the past, soon found that the task led them to use their critical and rational powers to create a new individual synthesis. In non-literate society, of course, there are usually some individuals whose interests lead them to collect, analyse and interpret the cultural tradition in a personal way; and the written records suggest that this process went considerably further among the literate elites of Egypt, Babylon and China, for example. But perhaps because in Greece reading and writing were less restricted to any particular priestly or administrative groups, there seems to have been a more thorough-going individual challenge to the orthodox cultural tradition in sixth-century Greece than occurred elsewhere, Hecataeus, for example, proclaimed at about the turn of the century, "what I write is the account I believe to be true. For the stories the Greeks tell are many and in my opinion ridiculous," and offered his own rationalizations of the data on family traditions and lineages which he had collected. Already the mythological mode of using the past, the mode which, in Sorel's words, makes it "a means of acting on the present, has begun to disappear.

That this trend of thought had much larger implications can be seen from the fact that the beginnings of religious and natural philosophy are connected with similar critical departures from the inherited traditions of the past; as W.B. Yeats wrote, with another tradition in mind, "Science is the critique of myths, there would be no Darwin had there been no *Book* of Genesis." Among the early pre-Socratics there is much evidence of the close connection between new ideas and the criticism of the old. Thus Xenophanes of Colophon (*fl.ca.* 540 B.C) rejected the "fables of men of old," and replaced the anthropomorphic gods of Homer and Hesiod who did "everything that is disgraceful and blameworthy among men" with a supreme god, "not at all like mortals in body and mind;'' while Heraclitus of Ephesus (*fl.ca.* 500 B.C., the first great philosopher of the problems of knowledge, whose system is based on the unity of opposites expressed in the *Logos* or structural plan of things, also ridiculed the anthropomorphism and idolatry of the Olympian religion.

The critical and sceptical process continued and according to Cornford, "a great part of the supreme god's biography had to be frankly rejected as false, or reinterpreted as allegory, or contemplated with reserve as mysterious myth too dark for human understanding." On the one had the poets continued to use the traditional legends for their poems and plays; on the other the prose writers attempted to wrestle with the problems with which the changes in the cultural tradition had faced them. Even the poets, however, had a different attitude to their material. Pindar, for example, used *mythos* is the sense of traditional stories, with the implication that they were not literally true; but claimed that his own poems had nothing in common with the fables of the past. As for the prose writers; and indeed some of the poets they had set out to replace myth with something else more consistent, with their sense of the *logos* of the common and all-encompassing truth which reconciles apparent contradictions.

From the point of view of the transmission of the cultural tradition the categories of understanding connected with the dimensions of time and space have a particular importance. As regards an objective description of space, Anaximander (b. 610 B.C.) and Hecataeus (*fl. ca.* 510-490), making use of Babylonian and Egyptian techniques drew, the first maps of the world. Then their crude beginnings were subject to a long process of criticism and correction—by Herodotus and others; and from this emerged the more scientific cartography of Aristotle, Eratosthenes and their successors.

The development of history appears to have followed a rather similar course, although the actual details of the process are subject to much controversy. The traditional view gave priority to local histories which were followed by the more universal accounts of Herodotus and Thucydides Dionysius of Halicarnasus writes of the predecessors of these historians who "instead of coordinating their accounts with each other...treated of individual peoples and cities separately.... They all had the one same object to bring to the general knowledge of the public the written records that they found preserved in temples or in secular buildings in the form in which they found them, neither adding nor taking away anything; among these records were to be fond legends hallowed by the passage of time....."

Jacoby however has insisted "the whole idea is wrong that Greek historiography began with local history. As far as Athens is concerned history begins with the foreigner Herodotus who, not long after the middle of the fifth century, incorporated parts of the story of the town in his work because he wanted to explain the role it played in the great conflict between East and West, between Europe and Asia. The aim of Herodotus' *History* was to discover what the Greeks and persians "fought each other for;" and his method was *histortia*—personal inquiry or research into the most probable versions of events as they were to be fond in various sources. His work rested on oral tradition and consequently his writings retained many mythological elements. So too did the work of the logographer Hellanicus of Lesbos, who at the end of the fifth century wrote the first history of Attica from 683 to the end of the

Peloponnesian war in 404. Hellanicus also tried to reconstruct the genealogies of the Homeric forwards heroes, both backwards to the Gods and to the Greece of his own time; and this inevitably involved chronology the objective measurement of time. All he could do, however, was to rationalize and systematize largely legendary materials. The development of history as a documented and analytic account of the past and present of the society in permanent written from took an important step forward with Thucydides, who made a decisive distinction between myth and history a distinction to which little attention is paid in non-literate society. Thucydides wanted to give a wholly reliable account of the wars between Athens and Sparta; and this meant that unverified assumptions about the past had to be excluded. So Thucydides rejected, for example, the chronology that Hellanicus had worked out for the prehistory of Athens, and confined himself very largely to his own notes of the events and speeches he related, or to the information he sought out from eye-witnesses and other reliable sources.

And so, not long after the widespread diffusion of writing throughout the Greek world, and the recording of the previously oral cultural tradition there arose an attitude to the past very different from that common in non-literate societies. Instead of the unobtrusive adaptation of past tradition to present needs a great many individuals found in the written records, where much of their traditional cultural repertoire had been given permanent form, so many inconsistencies in the beliefs and categories of understanding handed down to them that they were impelled to a much more conscious comparative and critical, attitude to the accepted world picture, and notably to the notions of God, the universe and the past. Many individual solutions to these problems were themselves written down, and these versions formed the basis for further investigations.

In non-literate society it was suggested, the cultural tradition function as a series of interlocking face-to-face conversations in which the very conditions of transmission operate to favor consistency between past and present, and to make criticism—the articulation of inconsistency—less likely to occur; and if it does, the inconsistency makes a less permanent impact, and is more easily adjusted or forgotten. While scepticism may be present in such societies it tales a personal, non-cumulative form; it does not lead to a deliberate rejection and reinterpretation of social dogma so much as to a semi-automatic readjustment of belief.

In literate society these interlocking conversations go on; but they are no longer man's only dialogue; and insofar as wiring provides as alternative source for the transmission of cultural orientations it favors awareness of inconsistency. One aspect of this is a sense of change and of cultural lag; another is the notion that the cultural inheritance as a whole is composed of two very different kinds of material; fiction, error and superstition on the one hand ; and on the other, elements of truth which can provide the basis for some more reliable and coherent explanation of the gods, the human past and the physical world.

Summary

Recent anthropology has rightly rejected the categorical distinctions between the thinking of "primitive" and "civilized" peoples, between 'mythopoeic" and "logico-empirical" modes of thought. But the reaction has been pushed too far; diffuse relativism and sentimental egalitarianism combine to turn a blind eye on some of the most basic problems of human history. Where the intellectual differences in the cultural traditions of complex and simple societies are given adequate recognition, the explanations offered are unsatisfactory. In the case of Western civilization, for example, the origins are sought in the nature of the Greek genius, in the grammatical structure of the Indo-European languages, or somewhat more plausibly in the technological advances of the Bronze Age and the associated developments in the division of labor.

In our view, however, insufficient attention has been paid to the fact that the urban revolution of the Ancient Near East produced one invention, the invention of writing, which changed the whole structure of the cultural tradition. Potentially, human intercourse was now no longer restricted to the impermanency of oral converse.

But since the first methods of writing employed were difficult to master, their effects were relatively limited and it was only when the simplicity and flexibility of later alphabetic writing made widespread literacy possible that for the first time there began to take concrete shape in the Greek world of the 7th century B.C. a society that was essentially literate and that soon established many of the institutions that became characteristic of all later literate societies.

The development of an easy system of writing (easy both in terms of the materials employed and the signs used) was more than a mere pre-condition of the Greek achievement; it influenced its whole nature and development in fundamental ways. In oral societies the cultural tradition is transmitted almost entirely by face--to-face communication; and changes in its content are accompanied by the homeostatic process of forgetting or transforming those parts of the tradition that cease to be either necessary or relevant. literate societies on the other hand, cannot discard absorb, or transmute the past in the same way. Instead their members are faced with permanently recorded versions of the past and its beliefs; and because the past is thus set apart from the present, historical enquiry becomes possible. This in turn encourages scepticism; and scepticism, not only about the legendary past, but about received ideas about the universe as a whole. From here the next step is to see how to build up and to test alternative explanations; and out of this there arose the kind of logical, specialized, and cumulative intellectual tradition of sixth-century Ionia. The kinds of analysis involved in the syllogism and in the other forms of logical procedure are clearly dependent upon writing, indeed upon a form of writing sufficiently simple and cursive to make possible widespread and habitual recourse both to the recording of verbal statements and then to the dissecting of them. It is probable that it is only the analytic process that writing itself entails, the written formalization of sounds and syntax, which make possible the habitual separating out into formally distinct units of the various cultural elements whose indivisible wholeness is the essential basis of the "mystical participation" which Levy-Bruhl regards as characteristic of the thinking of non-literate peoples.

One of the problems which neither Levy-Bruhl nor any other advocate of a radical dichotomy between "primitive" abd "civilized" thought has been able to resolve is the persistence of "non-logical thinking "in modern literate societies. But, of course, we must reckon with the fact that in our civilization writing is clearly an addition, not an alternative, to oral transmission. Even in our *buch und lesen* culture, childrearing and a multitude of other forms of activity both within and outside the family depend upon speech; and the relationship between the written and the oral traditions must be regarded as a major problem in Western cultures.

A consideration of the consequences of literacy in these terms, then, throws some light not only upon the nature of the Greek achievemenc but also upon the intellectual differences between simple and complex societies. There are, of course, many other consequences we have not discussed—for instance, the role of writing in the running of centralized states and others bureaucratic organizations; our aim has only been to discuss in very general terms some of the more significant historical and functional consequences of literacy.

15

Academic Performance in Comprehensive Schools

Two Types of School Structure—Two Educational Philosophies

The "enrollment explosion" at the secondary school level and the expanded admission to the university-preparing school as well as to the university itself has given rise to questions about the "standard" of the students processed through a system of mass education as compared to an elitist one. The present author has deal with the problem of comprehensiveness versus elitism in other connections (Husen, 1962 and 1973). Suffice it to indicate here that the criteria of "standard" are not as self-evident as they might seem *prima facie*, simply because the comprehensive system is based partly on other values than the elitist and therefore cannot be evaluated according to identical criteria. The very term "standard" has had a time-honoured place in educational folklore. The danger of "lowered standards" had often been pointed out by those who oppose broadening access to advanced education.

One of the problems singled out for particular analysis in the survey research conducted by the International Association for the Evaluation of Educational Achievement (IEA) has for a long time been a central policy issue in Europe, namely whether and the extent to which a comprehensive school system should replace the prevailing selective one. The IEA Project provided an unprecedented opportunity to compare what happens to the superior students when upper secondary school enrollment is broadened. The reason for the passion that often has gone into the debate on the comprehensive versus the selective school is that it is not merely didactic principles or methods of organizing the curriculum that are at issue. At the heart of the matter we find two opposing educational philosophies reflecting strong vested interests. On one hand, we have the egalitarian and reconstructivist view, and on the other, the by and large conservative and elitist view of the educational system.

A comprehensive system provides a publicity supported school education for all children of mandatory school age in a given catchment area. This means that all programs or curricular offering are provided in the same school unit. Another essential feature of comprehensive is that no differentiation or grouping practices that definitively determine the ensuing educational and occupational careers are employed. Children from all walks of life are taken care of.

In a selective system children are by means of organizational differentiation at an early age allocated to different types of school, and, also at an early stage of their school career, grouping practices are employed aiming at spotting those who are supposed to be particularly academically oriented. Apart from selective admission and grouping, the system is as a rule also characterized by a high attrition rate in terms of grade-repeating and drop-out.

In the debate on the relative merits and drawbacks of the two systems it has been maintained, on the one hand, that the top pupils in a comprehensive system will suffer by having to be taught together with their more slow-learning peers. This will impair their standard of achievement in comparison with pupils of equal intellectual standing in systems where an organizational differentiation in terms of selection for separate academically oriented schools takes place at an early age or where strict homogeneous grouping within the school is employed.

The adherents of comprehensive education, on the other hand, maintain that the top pupils will not suffer as much in their systems as the great mass of the less academically-oriented students in a selective system, particularly those who rather early are left in the elementary school after the "book-oriented" have been selected for the university-preparing secondary schools.

The elitists maintain that a system of selection based on fair and equally employed criteria of excellence will open the avenues to high-status occupation to those from all walks of life who deserve it by possessing the necessary (mainly inherited) talent. The comprehensivists counter by claiming that a selective system is beset with a greater social bias than the comprehensive one. As one moves up the ladder of the formal educational system the proportion of lower-class pupils is mush lower in a selective than in a comprehensive system, which is interpreted as evidence for bias.

The two propositions, both the one on the standard of the elite and one on social bias, were tested on national systems of education in the first two large-scale surveys conducted by IEA (Husen, 1967; Postlewaite, 1967; Comber and Keeves, 1973). The national systems of education differ tremendously with regard to the size of the pre-university group (in per cent of the relevant age groups). In the mathematics study this group varied from less than 10 per cent in some European countries to more than 70 per cent in the United States. In the Science study (stage 2) the variation was by and large of the same order of magnitude. The variability in Europe had, however, decreased somewhat. Evidently, there is no point in making comparisons between mean performances behind which there are school populations representing such variations in terms of the proportion of the relevant age group. Thus, it was decided to take advantages of the IEA survey data for Population 4, that is to say, pupils who are in the terminal grade of the pre-university school. Typical national illustrations of this population are for instance the *Oberprimaner* in Germany, the pupils who are about to sit for the GCEA-level in England, and for the *baccalaureate* in France.

The problem of "comparing" the terminal pupils is not as simple as it might appear from the popular debate on the relative "standard" of secondary systems with a rather strict selection versus those with an open door policy. The problem of whether the one or the other system is to be preferred is a matter of what criteria one wants to employ in evaluating them, and therefore in the last run a question of political preferences. Even if the evaluators can agree upon what criteria should be employed, they will certainly put them in different orders of priority. The adherent of an elitist system tends to evaluate the schools in terms of the quality of their *end-products* either leaving out those who are lost in the selection and/or attrition process or attaching a lower priority to their educational fate. The comprehensivist prefers to look at what happens to the great mass of students. His overriding question is : How many are brought how far ?

Standard of the Elite in Mathematics

In what follows we shall focus on the standard of the elite in the industrialized IEA countries, using as our criteria achievements in mathematics and science at the pre-university level. The national systems which have been studied vary considerably with regard to retention rate or "holding power" at the upper secondary level. The high school seniors consist of some 75 per cent of the relevant age group in the United States, those who finish *gymnasium* as continuation school in Sweden (grades 11 and 12) are some 45 percent of the age group, the *Oberprimaner* (grade 13) in the Federial Republic of Germany are some 10 percent etc. It is rather pointless to limit a comparison of student achievement in these and other countries to mean performances, simply because of the highly variable portion of the relevant age group we are dealing with. It is more nearly fair to compare *equal portions* of the age cohorts.

But such comparisons are conducted under the assumption that those who are *not* in school at that age level have not, either by previous schooling or other learning opportunities, reached the level of competence achieved by the elite still in school. On the basis of analysis of the distributions of achievements, both at the beginning and at the end of secondary school, we concluded that had the ideal conditions of being able to test the entire age group existed those who were not in school would not have scored high enough to affect the means for the top 5 per cent of the age group.

The objection has been raised that the method of comparing equal portions of the age group is unfair to national systems with a low retention rate (or high selectivity). The validity of such an objection can be questioned on pure logical grounds, simply because it is not consistent with the elitist philosophy. In systems where until recently only some 5-15 per cent of the entire age group is retained up to the pre-university grade, the prevailing educational philosophy has been that such a system rather efficiently takes care of most of the able pupils and does not bias against any category of them. Thus, those who favour an elitist system cannot reasonably object to a comparison between equal proportions of the age group by maintaining that

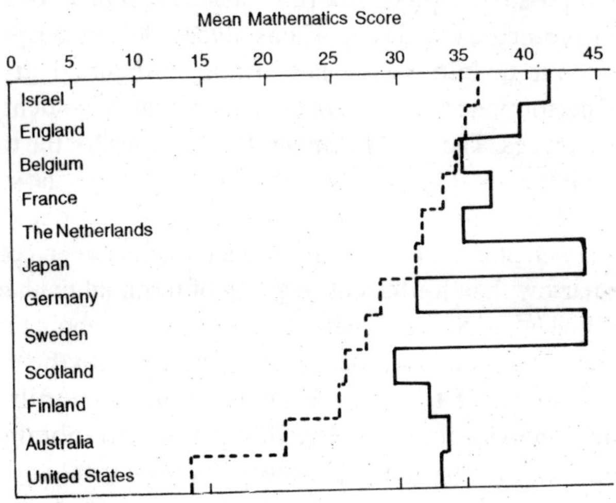

Figure 1. *Mean Mathematics Test Scores* (1) *for the Total Sample and* (2) *for Equal Proportion of Age Group in Each Country for Terminal Mathematics Populations*

____ Average mathematics test score for equal proportions of age groups

_ _ _ Average mathematics test score for country

Source: T. Husen (Ed.): International Study of Achievement in Mathematics: A Comparison Between, Twelve Countries. New York: Wiley, 1967.

the comparison is unfair to the selective system because it does not retain the able pupils. There is, however, a valid statistical objection. Harnqvist (1974) in reviewing the IEA surveys in Science, reading the literature points out that the errors of measurement contribute to an overestimation of the size standard of the elite in comprehensive systems and conversely to an underestimation in selective systems.

When in the IEA mathematics study (Husen, 1967) the average performances in different countries of terminal students taking mathematics was compared, we found that the US high school graduates were far below the other countries. However, in the US 18 per cent of the age group of 17-18 year olds took mathematics as compared to 4-5 per cent in some European countries. In order to arrive at an answer to the question to what extent it is possible to produce an elite in a comprehensive system, one has to compare equal proportions of the relevant age group in the respective countries. The dotted line in Figure 1 gives the average performance of the terminal mathematics student in the twelve countries. The solid line gives the averages for the top four percent of the total age group. This percentage was selected because it represented the lowest proportion in any one country taking mathematics. As can be seen, the range between countries is more narrow than for the entire group of terminal mathematics pupils. The United States' top four percent score at about the same level as the corresponding group in other countries.On the basis of the distribution of total score of the terminal pupils in all countries, international percentile norms were obtained. In Figure 2 we have given the percentage of the total age group within each country which has reached the standard of the upper tenth of the terminal mathematics pupils. As can be seen, none of the systems with high retention rates and/or a comprehensive structure are among the five systems at the bottom.

Standard of the Elite in Science

Similar comparisons were conducted with terminal students in science (Comber and Keeves, 1973). In this case all the population

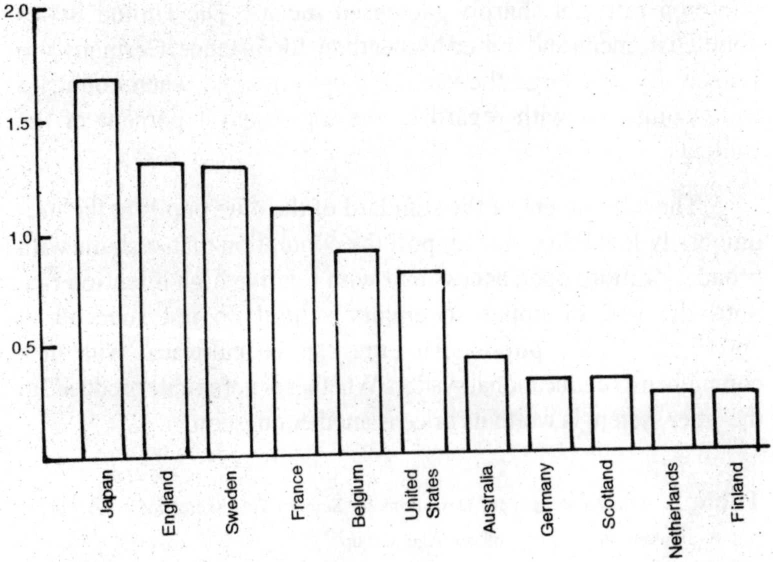

Figure 2. ***Percent of Age Group Reaching Upper Tenth of Terminal Mathematics Pupils by International Standards***

Source: T. Husen (Ed.): International Study of Achievement in Mathematics: A Comparison Between Twelve Countries. New York: Wiley, 1967.

4 pupils were included in the comparisons, irrespective of whether they were or were not taking science in the grade when testing took place. It was decided to compare the top 9 per cent of population 4 in the industrialized countries. This percentage was chosen because it represented the lowest proportion in population 4 of the relevant age group in any of the countries. In order to arrive at measures of two more limited sites, the top 5 and 1 per cent were also chosen. Table 1 and Figure 3 percent the outcomes of the comparisons for the three elite groups. The means score for the entire graduate population ranges from 30.8 for New Zealand to only 14.2, for the United States. As can be seen in Table 1, the Population 4 pupils represent 13 percent of the entire age group in the former country as compares to 75 in the latter. When the mean scores for the top

9 percent were compared, it was found that countries with a high retention rate got sharply increased means. The United States doubled its mean and scored higher than, for instance, Germany and France. By and large the same picture emerged when countries were compared with regard to the top 5 and 1 percent of the students.

The assessment of the standard of the elite pupils at the pre-university level does not support the contention that systems with broader or more open access and with relative high retention rate until the end of upper secondary school do not succeed in "producing" elite pupils. An elite can be cultivated with in a comprehensive educational system. Whether or not an elite produced in the latter system is worth its price is another question.

Table 1. Means and Standard Deviations for Science Test Scores for Total Sample and Equivalent Proportions of an Age Group

	% at		Full sample		Top 1%		Top 5%		Top 9%	
Country	School	N	Mean	SD	Mean	SD	Mean	SD	Mean	SD
New Zealand	13	1,676	30.8	12.6	52.8	2.8	43.5	5.9	36.8	9.0
England	20	2,181	24.4	12.4	51.6	3.2	41.6	6.5	35.5	8.5
Australia	29	4,194	26.1	11.5	51.5	3.2	44.0	4.7	39.9	5.9
Scotland	17	1,321	24.4	12.9	50.7	3.8	40.6	6.4	34.4	8.7
Sweden	45	2,754	20.1	10.9	49.5	3.4	41.2	5.3	37.0	6.2
Hungry	28	2,828	24.0	9.6	48.0	3.8	39.0	5.4	35.0	6.1
Netherlands	13	1,138	24,4	12.0	47.1	3.6	37.2	6.5	30.3	9.4
Finland	21	1,725	20.8	10.5	46.0	4.1	35.7	6.4	30.7	7.4
USA	75	2,514	14.2	9.9	45.8	2.8	36.8	5.5	33.1	5.9
FRG	9	1,989	28.4	9.6	45.0	4.1	35.3	6.2	28.4	9.6
France	29	3,523	19.1	9.1	40.5	3.5	33.3	4.4	29.9	5.1
Belgium (Fl)	47	467	18.1	8.5	39.8	3.7	33.0	4.0	30.5	4.2
Italy	16	15,719	16.5	9.2	38.2	4.7	27.4	6.5	22.7	7.3
Belgium (Fr)	47	941	16.0	8.3	36.2	2.0	30.9	3.1	28.4	3.7
Average			22.0		45.9		37.1		32.3	
Range			16.6		16.6		16.6		17.2	
Chile	16	1,947	9.3	6.3	23.5	3.8	16.8	4.3	13.6	4.8
India	14	3,040	6.3	6.1	20.8	3.7	12.8	4.8	9.5	5.2
Iran	9	1,051	10.8	5.9	21.9	3.6	14.8	4.4	10.8	5.9
Thailand	10	724	12.5	6.1	23.2	2.4	17.4	3.6	13.6	5.3

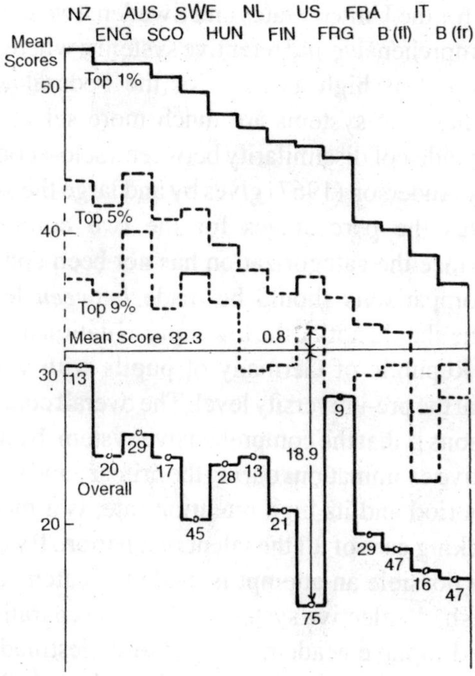

Figure 3. Science Mean Scores of Top 1%, Top 5%, Top 9% of an Age-Group and of Overall Group.

Source: L,C, Comber and John P. Keeves: Science Education in Nineteen Countries. Stockholm and New York : Almqvist & Wiksell and Wiley-Halsted Press, 1973.

In selective systems the high standard of the elite is often bought at the price of limiting opportunities of the mass of the pupils. By comparing the distribution of father's occupation at the 14-years-old level with the one of the pre-university level, it is possible within each country to arrive at an estimation of the amount of social selection that operates between the two levels. An index of social disproportion of pupils with fathers who belonged to the professional and managerial category on one hand and the semi-skilled or unskilled category on the other. The index was unity when the upper and lower strata have the same representation at the pre-university level as at the 14 years old level. The index was 1.3 and 2.4 respectively for the United States and Sweden, two countries with relatively comprehensive and retentive systems; whereas it was 7.9 for England and as high as 37.7 for the Federal Republic of Germany, where the systems are much more selective and less retentive. An index of dissimilarity between socio-economic strata developed by Anderson (1967) gives by and large the same results. Table 2 gives the percentages for the two contrasted status categories. Since the categorization has not been consistent over countries, comparisons should be made *between* levels within countries. One should notice the low representation in England and the Federal Republic of Germany of pupils with working class background at the pre-university level. The overall conclusion from the comparisons is that the comprehensive system, by its openness, lack of selective examinations during the primary and initial secondary school period and its high retention rate, is a more effective strategy in taking care of all the talent of a nation. By casting a net as widely as possible an attempt is made to "catch" an optimum number of fish. A selective system with early separation of pupils who are rated to have academic potential is destined to produce good end products. But this advantage is bought at the high price of excluding a sizable number of pupils from lower class homes from further education and of limiting the opportunities for the great mass of pupils to get access to quality education.

Table 2. Percentage of Pupils Within Each Population From Selected Categories of Parental Occupation.

	Population I (10 years-olds)		*Population II (14 years olds)*		*Population IV (17-19 years olds)*	
	Professional & managerial	*Unskilled & semi-skilled workers*	*Professional & managerial*	*Unskilled &semi-skilled workers*	*Professional & managerial*	*Unskilled & semi skilled workers*
England	16	21	14	14	38	5
Fed. Rep. of Germany	13	7	14	8	49	1
Finland	9	35	10	34	20	15
Hungry	15	43	20	36	38	18
Netherlands	26	12	20	12	55	5
Sweden	23	31	26	27	35	15
USA	24	18	31	16	34	14

Source: L.C. Comber and John P. Keeves: Science Education in Nineteen Countries. Stockholm and New York: Almqvist & Wiksell and Wiley-Halsted Press, 1973.